Praise for *Roar*

"By the pivotal nature of his work, which bridges the artificial divides of North and South, Buddhist and non-Buddhist, self and other, bringing a healthy mix of universalism and concern for local culture, and by the exemplary courage he has manifested in 'speaking truth to power,' Sulak Sivaraksa has made, and continues to make, a major contribution to peace and justice in his native Thailand, as well as in the world as a whole."

— Mairead Maguire, Nobel Peace Prize Laureate from Northern Ireland

"[Sulak] is an old friend and an inspiring, amazing figure in world Buddhism. *Roar* offers a marvelous and compelling story of his courage and audacity, of [Sulak's] extraordinary place in the modern history of Thailand, and his creative, feisty, unstoppable force of compassion and wisdom."

— Jack Kornfield, author of *No Time Like the Present*

"[Sulak] is one of the heroes of our time, offering us deep wisdom and re-freshingly sane alternatives to the earth-destroying religions of consumer-ism, greed, and exploitation."

— Joanna Macy, author of *World as Lover, World as Self*

"An irrepressible campaigner for a sane and just society, [Sulak] unites the strengths of a traditional Dharmic sensibility with the critical rigor of a West-ern-educated intellectual. His life offers a heroic example of engaged Bud-dhism in practice."

— Stephen Batchelor, author of *Secular Buddhism*

"In the entire world I know of no one who understands the situation more clearly and acts more effectively and consistently to bring the resources of a great religious tradition to bear on the critical issues of our time than Sulak Sivaraksa. I wish I could point to equally effective Christian leaders. I cannot. But perhaps we Christians can be inspired by him and learn from him and can find the strength to act creatively."

    —John B. Cobb, Jr., author of *A Christian Natural Theology*

"The question of alternatives to the current economic model has become extremely urgent.... Sulak Sivaraksa has been in the forefront of developing a thoroughgoing critique of consumerism."

    —Walden Bello, author of *Capitalism's Last Stand?*

"Whenever I ask myself a basic question of public ethics and public action, I end up wondering what [Sulak] would think. He has that great virtue of being true to himself and to the standards which somehow link all great moral philosophies.... [Sulak] is an unstoppable force working on justice from a Buddhist point of view."

    —John Ralston Saul, author of *The Collapse of Globalism and the Reinvention of the World*

Roar

Roar

Sulak Sivaraksa and the Path of Socially Engaged Buddhism

Matteo Pistono

Foreword by **John Ralston Saul**
Afterword by **Harsha Navaratne**

North Atlantic Books
Berkeley, California

Published by
North Atlantic Books   Cover art by Nathaniel Russell
Berkeley, California   Printed in the United States of America

The cover image was drawn by Nathaniel Russell and is a rendering of the lion atop the Ashokan pillar in Sarnath, near the site of the Buddha's enlightenment. The Emperor Ashoka ruled over much of the Indian subcontinent in the third century BCE and who, after converting to Buddhism, erected thousands of Ashokan pillars with edicts of religious tolerance and non-violence. The "Roar" of a lion is a metaphor used by the Buddha to express the fearlessness needed to teach the Dharma, as well as the potency of the teachings themselves that result in enlightenment

Roar: Sulak Sivaraksa and the Path of Socially Engaged Buddhism is sponsored and published by the Society for the Study of Native Arts and Sciences (dba North Atlantic Books), an educational nonprofit based in Berkeley, California, that collaborates with partners to develop cross-cultural perspectives, nurture holistic views of art, science, the humanities, and healing, and seed personal and global transformation by publishing work on the relationship of body, spirit, and nature.

North Atlantic Books' publications are available through most bookstores. For further information, visit our website at www.northatlanticbooks.com or call 800-733-3000.

Library of Congress Cataloging-in-Publication data
is available from the publisher upon request.

1 2 3 4 5 6 7 8 9 KPC 24 23 22 21 20 19

Printed on recycled paper

North Atlantic Books is committed to the protection of our environment. We partner with FSC-certified printers using soy-based inks and print on recycled paper whenever possible.

Also by Matteo Pistono:

In the Shadow of the Buddha: One Man's Journey of Discovery in Tibet

Fearless in Tibet: The Life of the Mystic Tertön Sogyal

Meditation: Coming to Know Your Mind

Dedication from Sulak Sivaraksa and Matteo Pistono

To Lodi Gyari Rinpoche, our kalyanamitta and our guru—
the wise, most broad-minded, and the best.

Contents

Photo Credits

All other photos courtesy of the library of Sulak Sivaraksa.
For photos that are not credited, the photographer is unknown.

Foreword

John Ralston Saul,
Past president of PEN International

There is nothing romantic about ethics. It is a muscle. The more you use it, the stronger it gets. And in that process life reveals to each of us how much we can develop this quality; how strong it can become.

Whenever I write about ethics I think of Sulak Sivaraksa. I wonder when it was that he—a most conscious person—realized what kind of life he was going live. What kind of person he really was. What kind of person he was going to become. It can't have been all that clear at first. Training to be a barrister in London would have confused many, particularly an outsider. Empires develop cultures which are both seductive in method and superior in attitude. They aim to draw the outsider in as a way of undermining their sense of themselves. An imperial education is always a constant test for the outsider. A few come out stronger, more independent, pre-maturely conscious of the drama which each of our lives represents. Sulak was one of those.

There is another particularity about Sulak. He belongs to that rare group of deeply ethical activists who have made themselves. I don't mean that in the conventional sense of economics or ambition. Some people are shoved by birth or career into ethical crises that they cannot escape. They might be reincarnated into a role or born or promoted into it as spiritual leaders or royal figures or political chiefs. Suddenly they find themselves staring into a mirror of ethical choice. All positions of responsibility come equipped with an ethical mirror. They cannot escape it. They have to choose again and again. And the citizenry or worshippers outside the room of responsibility will make of these choices what they can. As will history. You might call this the existentialism of power and responsibility.

Sulak belongs to another breed, a rare breed. Not necessarily better. But rarer. People like him are not trapped into ethical choices by their position. They move toward their ethical soul as if alone, as if propelled by fate or by their own character. And in so doing they become a reference point for others. A model. This is not an easy role. Much of it is played out in full public view, yet you have no institutional cover. You are exposed. Always alone.

There are never many of these people among the living. I am lucky enough to know a few, including Sulak. This role, at first glance, seems to contain a contradiction—between the toughness needed for the public place and the modesty needed for spirituality. Someone like Sulak must live on that thin, fragile line. He must speak out. People need him to be seen and heard. This is, in fact, a profound forum of modesty as it involves constantly risking everything. The nonviolent movement, of which Sulak is an important part, exemplifies this. It is not about passivity. It is action. It is all about walking up to the line, crossing it if necessary, being there at the heart of a cause. In his address to the courtroom in 1995, at the end of a two-and-a-half-year legal battle in which the military tried once again to destroy him, he said, "The essence of being a human is having the courage to confront truth without pretension."

I often think of another moment, when Sulak felt he could only express his opposition to a Myanmar/Thai pipeline by making his way into the construction camp in the northern jungle in order to sit down in its path; he, a distinguished, elderly, revered public figure. The police arrived and reluctantly arrested him. But he refused to get into their air-conditioned car, and they certainly didn't want to put their hands on him. So Sulak walked the many kilometers to the police station, with a police car on either side, doors open, as they tried to cool him with their air conditioning.

Humor is always present in Sulak's methodology. But so is his sense that action alone can do very little. People must change themselves. They must battle the three poisons of greed, anger/hatred and delusion. And while Buddhism asks a great deal in this way of the individual, Sulak insists that we must also recognize an additional factor of enormous importance: the extent to which social structures block individual change. Yes, we must each find ways to change ourselves. But that is not enough. If we simply walk away to face our personal drama, the injustices of society will remain in place, and our absence will have the effect of indifference before the suffering of others.

I will always remember opening the first page of *Seeds of Peace*, the first line: "Western consumerism is the dominant ethic in the world today." Sulak is not complaining about the false comfort of public life or waxing romantic about simpler ways. What he is saying is that the Buddhist precepts of not killing, not stealing, not abusing sexually, are all violated by the system of Western consumerism.

The point here is not simple. It is multifaceted. Sulak lives his life in a certain way, as a follower of Bhikkhu Buddhadasa, seeking a simple form of life in the midst of his complex engagement.

However, he also bases his actions on words. Arguments. He is a thinker, a wordsmith. His actions must emerge from intellectual and existential realities. This allows him to work out what brings things together. On top of that, he is devoted to the importance of local culture. This is the reality of people's lives. He follows Buddhadasa's principles of turning selfishness into the service of others, respecting our friends' religions as our own, and working with those friends to overcome materialism and the dominance of economics. Why? Because they lie at the heart of selfishness.

These various ideas may seem at first both unrelated and inoffensive. And yet because Sulak uses real language with real actions of self-engagement, he has been twice driven into exile, has been in prison, has lived a life of risk in opposition to corrupt power and what he would call selfishness. He is a man who uses action to advance words.

Yes, this life of his has provoked anger in those he opposes. Yet that anger merely reveals who they are. There is a persistence in Sulak, a long, long view. And a desire to bring people together. At the Festival of Ideas in Adelaide in 2001, he said, "There must be a spiritual component to reconciliation and this must occur in the individual, family, community and nation."

We have met repeatedly over the last thirty-five years. First at his house in Bangkok, in perhaps 1980, no air conditioning, screened and open with a fan blowing, as he talked of the need to approach the world differently. In Toronto during his second exile, when PEN Canada made him an honorary member. In Bangkok, in a celebratory mood, the day after the courts acquitted him in 1995. In Yangon celebrating his eighty-third birthday with his friends and admirers. And on and on. Each time I am struck by his ability to describe reality in an honest, tough way. But also by his wry humor, his persistence, that sense that we must all keep pushing because the cause is good. And in the midst of a world of violence, greed and consumerism, his determination to work for the good is always shaped by a strong sense of restraint. Things must change, but not by giving in to the poisons of those forces and habits and structures he seeks to alter. This requires determined restraint, but also great and constant strength. An intelligent and spiritual strength. Sulak remains, as he has always been, a model for a great number of people. He is certainly a model for the way I try to live my own life. There are many of us around the world who say the same thing.

Acknowledgments

Roar: Sulak Sivaraksa and the Path of Socially Engaged Buddhism is based upon extensive interviews I conducted with Ajahn Sulak Sivaraksa between 2011–2016. I am deeply appreciative of Ajahn Sulak who was generous with his time as he sat for many hours answering my questions, and for opening his vast network of friends and colleagues to me. We usually met in the open-air courtyard of his Bangkok home, but also at universities, activist gatherings, Buddhist temples, tea houses, and ashrams in the United States, India, and Sri Lanka. Thanks to Nilchawee, Ajahn Sulak's wife, who always made me feel comfortable during my stays in their home. The book benefited from the insights of seventy other individuals—professors, activists, students, monks, nuns, artists, Ajahn Sulak's family, and politicians—who I interviewed in Thailand, the United States, India, Japan, France, England and Germany. A deep bow of appreciation to each individual who helped me gain a more nuanced picture of the complex life and personality of Ajahn Sulak.

Deep appreciation goes to my wife, Monica Garry, for her support and love. Kendra Crossen Burroughs was immensely helpful with her editorial assistance. And thanks to my mother, Francey Pistono, for reviewing early drafts of this book.

Arnie Kotler, who published Ajahn Sulak's autobiography *Loyalty Demands Dissent* in 1998, escorted *Roar* through the last stages of publication, for which I'm very thankful. And to North Atlantic Books, thanks for recognizing the importance of the life story of Ajahn Sulak.

Roar was written for socially engaged spiritual practitioners around the world—may you find true *kalyana-mitta* along your path to awakening while working for the benefit of others in myriad ways!

Portrait of Sulak seated in his library with Prince
Damrong's cane.

Chapter 1

Born a Royalist

It was August 1991, and Sulak Sivaraksa, branded as a fugitive, was on the run. He had changed into the clothes of a villager of northern Thailand, so as to appear like the other locals who were bartering and selling wares along the border. He kept his hat pulled low over his face because his image had been broadcast over national TV. After slipping a bribe to a boatman to avoid the security checkpoint, Sulak crossed the Mekong River to Laos in a small canoe, undetected.

An arrest warrant for Sulak had been issued after he delivered a speech at Bangkok's Thammasat University, titled "The Regression of Democracy in Siam." General Suchinda Kraprayoon, the head of the government and military junta, charged Sulak with defamation of both King Bhumibol and himself.

Sulak took refuge inside the German embassy in Bangkok to evade authorities—a necessary step, since political dissidents, intellectuals, and journalists who opposed the military junta were being targeted, disappeared, and assassinated. Outside the embassy gates on Sathon Road, police cars waited for Sulak to appear. Plainclothes officers posted near his home in the center of the city monitored Sulak's many disciples who came to see his wife, who remained living there with their three children. Sulak kept in touch with his wide network of family, friends, activists, monks, and diplomats around the world. He solicited their advice on how he should proceed.

The crime of lèse-majesté—defamation of the monarchy—forbids criticism of the king, queen, crown prince, or regent, and in Thailand brings with it a fifteen-year prison sentence. After a two-week standoff at the embassy, Sulak called his wife and told her he had decided to surrender to the police and fight the general's charges in court. Pibhop Dhongchai, Sulak's closest disciple, had brought a reporter from the English-language Bangkok newspaper *The Nation* to document the arrest in front of the embassy. Word spread that Sulak was going to be arrested. Many of his admirers eagerly anticipated his resistance to the powers that be; they wanted their country to have its own Gandhi in the ever-vocal Sulak. Sulak's detractors, who were even more numerous than his supporters, especially among the elite and ruling class, looked forward to the silencing of the country's most prominent intellectual and moral critic.

But at the eleventh hour, the plan was changed. Instead of surrendering to police the next morning, Sulak dashed surreptitiously out an alleyway gate and ducked into an automobile that raced him to the border. A close confidant, Dr. Prawase Wasi, had persuaded him to flee. The Thai police and judicial system were unpredictable, and Sulak was in very real danger. "Don't be brave, Sulak," Dr. Prawase urged his friend. "They want to kill you. You must leave the country."

Taking back roads and sleeping in jungle safe houses, Sulak listened to radio broadcasts calling him a rat and a criminal. He paid triple the going water-taxi fare for the boatman to skirt him around the border checkpoint to cross the Mekong River into Laos. Sulak was on his own, with only a few hundred baht and a package of salty crackers in his satchel. Scared, he meditated on his breath to calm his mind as he rode a rickety bus and found his way to the home of sympathetic Laotian friends, the social rights campaigner Sombath Somphone and his wife, Shui-Meng Ng. Sombath was out of the country. Shui-Meng helped Sulak with secret communications back to Thailand and abroad as they planned how to have Sulak travel to the West. After Sulak had spent two days in hiding, Shui-Meng loaned him US $2,000 and arranged for him to board an Aeroflot flight using the boarding pass of a student en route to study abroad. When the plane touched down in Stockholm, Sulak called his wife, knowing the police had tapped his home telephone and were listening. He told her he was safe but did not know how long he would be in exile.

Throughout the Buddhist world, there are practitioners who regard their political work and their spiritual path as one and the same. Indeed, two of the most prominent global Buddhist leaders—the Dalai Lama and the Vietnamese Zen monk Thich Nhat Hanh—are both known for their lifelong pursuit of social justice and their practice of compassion in action. Another Buddhist leader is Aung San Suu Kyi, who returned to the world political stage after being released from fifteen years of house arrest by the Burmese military junta.

Violence and political strife in Tibet, Vietnam, and Burma have pushed the Dalai Lama, Thich Nhat Hanh, and Aung San Suu Kyi into greater roles and responsibility than they might otherwise have had. And like the work of these socially engaged Buddhists, Sulak's political activism, community organizing, and advocacy for marginalized people are an expression of his Buddhist practice.

Sulak has been exiled from Thailand on two occasions (in 1976–1977 and 1991–1992), jailed and harassed, and repeatedly subjected to criminal prosecution for defaming the Thai monarchy. He has always been acquitted. No one has been able to silence Sulak.

For more than forty years, Sulak has traveled the world, lecturing, writing, mentoring, participating in interreligious dialogues and conferences, and founding organizations such as the International Network of Engaged Buddhists, with his friends the Dalai Lama, Thich Nhat Hanh, and the late Ven. Maha Ghosananda as its patrons. With all this, he has also found time to establish scholarly journals, magazines, bookstores, and a publishing house for his own and other authors' works; more than a hundred books have appeared in Thai and English under his name.

Sulak's rise to worldwide prominence as a socially engaged Buddhist and an advocate for the oppressed, and his national celebrity as a thorn in the side of successive Thai governments and the monarchy, were unlikely for the son of a well-off Sino-Siamese family. This large family was assured financial stability and political security thanks to their connections with businesspeople who were loyal supporters of the country's Buddhist monarchy. Such a foundation would have provided Sulak with the education and societal connections needed to live comfortably on the periphery of Bangkok's elite circles. It was a position that any young man would have effortlessly embraced without questioning the status quo, for to do so would have endangered his personal wealth and comfortable life. But Sulak chose a different path.

Sulak was born on 27 March 1933, exactly nine months after a bloodless coup against King Prajadhipok, Rama VII, in 1932. The coup had been launched by a group of young intellectuals and military officers, many of whom had studied together in Paris in the 1920s. Pridi Banomyong, an idealistic university professor who was more a democrat than a revolutionary, led the overthrow of the absolute monarchy. Pridi and his People's Party were responsible for ending 150 years of the Chakri dynasty. Siam's first constitution was ratified, and Pridi promised that the land would be governed by the rule of law rather than by a king and a network of feudal lords and princes. The constitution introduced previously unknown ideas into society, for example that supreme power rests with the Siamese people and not the king or aristocrats. Out of respect for Siamese tradition, the People's Party allowed the king to retain his titular position but with no real power. Constitutional democracy had come to Siam, or so it was believed. That Sulak was born amid a period of political upheaval portended his emergence as a revolutionary character unlike anyone the country had ever produced.

A defining quality of Sulak's character, one that would endure throughout his life, was nurtured early on by the two most important male figures in his life—his father and his venerated Buddhist teacher. This quality was that of independent thinking.

Sulak's father, Chalerm, had been educated by French Catholics in Bangkok. Like many businessmen and those aspiring to enter the elite circles in the early 1900s in Siam, Chalerm idealized European culture. He spoke English and donned neckties and suits even in Bangkok's tropical heat. He earned a modest salary as an accountant employed by the British-American Tobacco Company.

In contrast, Sulak's mother's family had long-standing merchant ties with the rice trade that extended to China, which provided them access to Bangkok's aristocrats and Thailand's princes and princesses. The wealth the family accrued over generations, the sprawling multi-

Sulak, circa 1941, wearing the military-style uniform that the dictator Plaeak Phibunsongkram required schoolchildren to wear.

generational wooden compound with its orchards and gardens where Sulak played as a child, and the lifestyle of abundance did not last. When Sulak was five, his great-aunt Lom, the matriarch of the family, died, and disputes over the estate arose among the many siblings. Within a few years, nearly all of the family's property was sold or reclaimed by banks.

Sulak and his two elder half-brothers had lived with their father since the time Sulak was around six, owing to their parents' divorce. Chalerm remarried shortly after the divorce. He doted on his boys, especially Sulak. He trusted and confided in the young Sulak, speaking to him as if he were an adult, and the boy in turn reciprocated with adoration. Sulak recalls assimilating his father's conservative social and political views. Chalerm believed wholeheartedly in the absolute monarchy and preferred to live in a country ruled by those with royal blood rather than by democrats and the commoners who had recently risen to power. Sulak was imbued with skepticism of politicians, progressive monks, and promoters of democracy, including the likes of Pridi, the architect of the 1932 political revolution.

Sulak's father wanted his sons to have a European education, and Sulak was sent to an Anglican elementary school, St. Mary's. The school was a short walk from his home, past a Buddhist temple and along one of the many canals that give Bangkok its distinctive character. Chalerm was delighted that automobiles and telephone lines were beginning to weave themselves around the traditional teak houses, ancient gilded pagodas, and distinctive multitier temples of Bangkok. He wanted his son to grow up to be a modern man. At school Sulak enjoyed the catechism and going to chapel every day with the teachers, though he quarreled with them because he felt he was smarter than they were. This friction with his teachers was a preview of Sulak's lifelong clashes with authority figures.

Sulak's early education coincided with continued political upheaval and a struggle over the direction the country should take. The progressive Pridi had led the country since the 1932 revolution, but six years later his power was usurped by a fellow revolutionary, Plaeak Phibunsongkram. They continued to battle one another for political power for years.

Plaeak Phibunsongkram, known as Phibun, was Pridi's opposite. Pridi was a reserved and articulate academic who admired European social democrats. Phibun, a military man, admired fascism and had translated Hitler's and Mussolini's writings into Thai. Pridi wanted to use his intellectual brilliance in ways to serve others, while Phibun wanted to use his Machiavellian skills to consolidate power. After pushing Pridi aside in 1938, Phibun led the country as an ultranationalist prime minister until 1944, and again from 1948 to 1957.

Phibun identified a wide range of enemies of the state, including the princes, the old nobility, and immigrants. He decreed that the country would be entirely Buddhist, and he barred Muslims and Christians from entering civil service. He prohibited sarongs, village knickers, Manchu-style jackets, and other traditional clothing, and issued a government mandate for public attire to be Western trousers and skirts. Phibun commissioned a racist national anthem, ordered the destruction of literature written in local dialects, and, for both bigoted and economic reasons, fostered suspicion of Chinese and immigrants—which is the reason Sulak's father was forced to concoct a new name out of his ancestral Chinese surname. He changed his Chinese-based surname Seaw-kasem to the acceptable Sanskritized *Siva*, and added *raksa* to make Sivaraksa.

"We were taught to hate all Chinese, except our fathers and grandfathers. We knew we were Chinese. But we were told that we were now Thai," Sulak recalls. "I have never felt Thai. I am Siamese."

Of all the ultranationalist and racist moves that Phibun made, it was his renaming of the country that Sulak most often cites to exemplify the deep crisis in Siamese identity. Phibun changed the name of the country in 1939 from Siam to Thailand on the model of Deutschland, or Germany, because of his admiration for Hitler's notion of a superior "Aryan" race. He imagined that the Thai-speaking people who predominated in his country were also a great race, despite the fact that for millennia the country had been a rich tapestry of ethnicities— Chinese, Laotian, Khmer, Malay, Karen, Mon, Muser, Akha, and many more. Sulak believes the name change to Thailand symbolizes the crisis of traditional Siamese Buddhist values. Eliminating a nation's name has a dehumanizing effect on the citizens, Sulak says, especially when its original name is replaced by a foreign-derived name. "Thailand" reeks of chauvinism and irredentism, and for this reason Sulak calls his country Siam.

Like other children during Phibun's dictatorship, Sulak and his brothers were required to wear brown military uniforms at their school, started the school day with marching drills to promote nationalism, and regularly had to participate in political rallies. Phibun pushed his fascist messaging deep into educational institutions and government bureaucracy, creating a cult of personality around himself. The nation saluted the new national flag and praised the dictator at 8 a.m. and 6 p.m. sharp daily. As a result of one of the marches to a rally to hear Phibun denounce the French annexation of part of Thailand, Sulak's elder brother collapsed from exhaustion and died soon thereafter. Sulak's father blamed Phibun and was forever scarred by the loss; Sulak's lifelong disdain for authoritarianism was born.

Phibun identified all nations outside the Axis camp as enemies of Thailand. He signed an alliance with the Empire of Japan in 1941, and the Japanese used Thailand as a base to fight the British in Burma and battle the Dutch in Indonesia. In 1942, Thailand declared war against the United States and Britain; however, Seni Pramoj, the Thai minister in Washington, DC, took the bold step of not delivering the declaration. Still, the same year, Bangkok became Command Central for Japan's Southeast Asian front, and Japanese troops were stationed throughout Thailand. British and American aircraft flying out of India bombed Bangkok (among other targets in Thailand) from 1942 to 1945. The first combat mission of America's Superfortress B-29 took out railways and ports, as well as Japanese military camps.

Sulak recalls hearing the heavy propellers of the massive B-29 bombers flying over the city. He was taught to take cover under his school desk. After his father's family heard bombs exploding near their home, Sulak was sent to live with his mother in the countryside. The separation from his father pained Sulak. His father spoiled him; with his mother, Sulak argued. "She was my alter ego, with a short temper, bossy, always organizing," Sulak said. "We were very similar in many ways."

When the Allied bombings began to target locations outside Bangkok, Sulak moved again, this time between the home of his mother and that of other relatives who lived farther away and worked in the rural rice fields. Sulak preferred to wander in the countryside rather than attend his new school. He found comfort in the villages among the keepers of the country's oral history rather than learning by rote in Christian classrooms. He attended the nightly folk dramas, learned traditional *khon* dance, and visited with storytellers who regaled their listeners under the palm trees of the open courtyards in the village temples.

One day, when Sulak was visiting his father back in Bangkok, one of the household's most trusted servants, Kim Liang, invited the young boy to accompany him into the city. Liang was like an uncle to

Sulak and they enjoyed each other's company. He was an opium addict and would go to the city to get his fix. Sulak's father worked at the country's tobacco monopoly, and Liang used to pinch a few cigarettes—which were scarce during the war—to trade for his drug. The opium dens were nestled in alleyways, hidden from the city's many Buddhist temples and palaces. Although children were barred from the dens, Liang managed to bring Sulak with him into this sordid world, where dozens of half-naked men, shining with perspiration, lay on wicker cots. Candles flickered on low tables and shadows danced on the wall while Sulak watched opium being brought out in a small casket, melted on a lamp, and then placed into long bamboo pipes. After a deep inhalation, the eyes of the users would roll back in their heads as they lay wrapped in a blanket of bliss. Though Sulak never tried opium, he loved the sweet smell of the drug as the addicts smoked it.

Sulak accompanied Liang to the opium dens just a few times, but they left a mark on him because it was where he was introduced to Buddhism. Sulak had not received a traditional Buddhist education at home. His father showed respect to monks and admired their Buddhist monarch, but he did not pray, meditate, or go to the temple. He was a businessman and did not devote much time to religion until the last year of his life, when he suffered from cancer and turned to faith out of concern for his fate.

"I learned my first Buddhist prayers in the opium dens, as well as mantras and magical incantations to summon spirits," Sulak recalls. This was not the Buddhism of scholars and meditators, but that of the common man.

Sulak was also fascinated by the tattoos on the bodies of the intoxicated men he saw lying about. This ancient art, inked with a bamboo pen, was believed to have magic powers, bestowing protection from snakebites, knife blades, and other sources of harm. Though Sulak wished to receive a tattoo while in the opium dens, he knew that his father, who idealized all that was modern and civilized, did not approve of a practice he thought was vulgar and primitive.

Sulak may have been introduced to Buddhism in unlikely surroundings; nonetheless, he soon took the traditional step of becoming a novice monk for a period of time—a month or two, or longer. School is interrupted while boys are in the monastery; then they resume school after their monkhood. Some young men in Thailand choose to stay in the monastery, become fully ordained, and remain for their whole life. But most remain only for enough time to satisfy their parents' desire for them to have some Buddhist education, and for the parents to accumulate positive merits from having a son live the virtuous life of a monk. Sulak was eager to become a novice monk, but his younger half-brother, Pravit, did not want to join. Sulak's father promised Pravit a new bicycle if he became a monk for a few months. Pravit stayed at the monastery just long enough to get the bike, while Sulak chose to remain.

The monastery was attached to the royally endorsed Wat Thongnopphakhun, where Sulak's father, ever the monarchist, wanted his sons to be monks. After arriving, Sulak and Pravit had their heads ceremonially tonsured, were given orange robes, and were assigned a small hut with one mattress, a sheet, and a mosquito net. They took the five vows common to lay Buddhists, and the additional five precepts of a *samanera*, or novice monk, which the Buddha prescribed more than 2,500 years ago. The total of ten *samanera* vows are as follows:

1. Refrain from killing.
2. Refrain from taking what is not given.
3. Refrain from sexual activity.
4. Refrain from lying.
5. Refrain from taking intoxicants.
6. Refrain from eating food after noon.
7. Refrain from singing, dancing, and attending entertainment performances.
8. Refrain from wearing perfume, cosmetics, and jewelry.
9. Refrain from sitting on high seats and sleeping on luxurious, soft beds.
10. Refrain from accepting or handling money.

Upon accepting the ten precepts, the boys entered into the ordained *sangha,* the community of Buddhist monastics. The vows brought a simplicity to life that suited Sulak, and he remembers feeling liberated by the vows rather than constrained in any way.

In the temple, Sulak felt that he was treated like an adult by the abbot, his teacher, and the other monks. Whereas at his Christian missionary school he had been spanked and condescended to, here he was addressed with no regard to class distinctions. It was not unlike the manner in which his father had always treated him.

Wat Thongnopphakhun's senior scholar, the venerated monk Phra Bhaddramuni, was assigned to be Sulak's teacher. "He really has been my only teacher in this life," Sulak recalls. "Everyone else has been a 'spiritual friend' [*kalyana-mitta*]."

Phra Bhaddramuni was a deeply conservative monk who, like Sulak's father, supported the king without reservation and bemoaned the country's move away from absolute monarchy to democracy with a constitutional monarch. Sulak cherished his position as a monk at a royal temple. Though Wat Thongnopphakhun was not a high-ranking royal temple, princes and princess would visit occasionally to see Phra Bhaddramuni because he was an eminent astrologer. Though Phra Bhaddramuni was stern and fierce with his students, he spoke to Sulak as to an equal, with softness and kindness. One of the first lessons imparted to Sulak was: "You must always do your best. Never settle for anything mediocre. Do not seek fame and riches. Instead, strive for excellency."

Sulak became Phra Bhaddramuni's attendant straightaway and served him by preparing his betel nut and tea, massaging him, and looking after administrative matters. While his teacher was resting during the day, Sulak cooled off by swinging from a large mango tree and swimming in the canal that ran in front of Phra Bhaddramuni's residence. When Phra Bhaddramuni awoke, Sulak pounded the betel nut that his teacher enjoyed chewing in the afternoon. Phra Bhaddramuni introduced his young acolyte to roasted oolong tea, for which Sulak acquired a lifelong appreciation. The teacher did not busy himself with activities outside the temple but preferred to remain in his open-air hut, relaxing on a floor mat, propped on a traditional wedge pillow as he sipped tea and read astrological treatises or Buddhist texts. He often suggested titles for Sulak to read, and the two sat for long hours with their respective books.

Sulak acquired a lifelong fondness for reading in an atmosphere of personal liberty, the freedom to choose what he wished to read. As a schoolboy he had been required by bossy teachers to read textbooks that he found boring. But at the temple Sulak could read whatever library books he chose, and he also enjoyed the volumes on Buddhism, history, and literature that Phra Bhaddramuni offered him. "I have loved books ever since," he says.

Sulak immersed himself in the complete works of Prince Damrong (1862–1943), an influential writer whose famous two-volume study *Our Wars with the Burmese: Thai-Burmese Conflict 1539–1767* strengthened the youth's nascent royalism. In it, Prince Damrong expounded on his rationale for upholding such absolutism and the sacredness of the monarchy. Sulak recalls that at Wat Thongnopphakhun, "I breathed the air of conservatism, or rather ultraconservatism, daily. Arch-conservative royalists from the old order frequented the temple to see my teacher. Ours was a great temple in large part because it was a very conservative, royal temple." It was just such conservative absolutism—centered on the Thai monarchy—that Sulak would later oppose, and be arrested for and exiled. But during his time as a monk, and indeed for the first thirty years of his life, Sulak would have defended his king to his last breath.

Sulak entered the curriculum for novice monks, which included daily alms rounds before dawn, sweeping of the monastic grounds, chanting of prayers in the temple, and reading Buddhist texts in Pali, the language of the Theravada scriptures. Even at his young age of twelve, Sulak was supposed to deliver religious sermons to the laypeople who visited the temple. "I was nervous about giving sermons, and I would stutter," he says. Phra Bhaddramuni consoled Sulak, saying, "'Remind yourself: *What I am about to say are the words of the Buddha; I am sounding the words of the Great Teacher.'* When I did that, all my fear of public speaking went away."

Buddhism was introduced to the region during the fifth century, but it was not a pure form of Theravada philosophy. Rather—in the words of Chris Baker and Pasuk Phongpaichit in *A History of Thailand*—it was contained "in a package of Indic gods" that did not clearly distinguish the various sects and traditions from one another. It was not until the thirteenth century that Theravada Buddhism arrived in a pure form, brought by Sri Lankan monks. Yet, once it had arrived, the Theravada teachings was infused with local practices and religious beliefs, including "roles for Hindu gods, notions of supernatural power often borrowed from tantric types of Buddhism, and folk beliefs in spirits," Baker and Phongpaichit write.

With the establishment of Theravada Buddhism, so began the lineage of Buddhist kings in Siam. Legend traces the lineage to the foundation of the kingdom of Ayutthaya in the fourteenth century. Today's Chakri dynasty began some four hundred years later with King Thongduang, Rama I. As the Chakri tradition developed, it blended the Buddhist notion of the righteous ruler (*dhammaraja*) with the Hindu idea of the omnipotent god-king (*devaraja*). King Chulalongkorn, Rama V, was perhaps the most strident of the early Chakri kings in his assertion of absolute monarchy. He wrote:

> The king rules absolutely at his own royal desire. There is nothing greater than this. The king has absolute power as (1) ruler over the realm and refuge for the people; (2) the source of justice; (3) the source of rank and status; (4) commander of the armed forces who relieves the people's suffering by waging war or conducting friendly relations with other countries. The king does no wrong. There is no power that can judge or punish him.

It was Chulalongkorn's version of an absolute Buddhist monarch that had been forced out with the 1932 revolution. However, not everyone in Siam agreed with the People's Party, including Sulak's father and his Buddhist teacher. Sulak inherited the view from his father and teacher that the country was better off with an absolute monarch as Siam's benevolent overlord.

Sulak felt immense gratitude to his teacher and for the royal temple where he studied. He relished accompanying Phra Bhaddramuni to the Marble Temple upon the occasion of a visit by King Ananda, Mahidol, Rama VIII. Sulak wanted to offer something back to his teacher and to his temple. Rather than simply praise what he liked or what was working well, Sulak's manner of expressing gratitude was to identify what was not working well and to correct it—this was in his character early in his life. Thus, for example, he took action when he perceived a problem at the temple. Early in the mornings, the monks would gather for prayers and meditation. The gathering hall was locked, and the key holder, a respected senior monk, repeatedly overslept, so that his lateness shortened the monks' time for prayer. After a few such incidents, Sulak objected to his truancy. The elderly monk responded with a swift knock on Sulak's head. "I was so angry, but I channeled my anger. I denounced him with written criticism and posted it on the temple walls, stating the facts and the need for punctuality." The senior monk was furious and threatened Sulak, but Phra Bhaddramuni protected his young acolyte from reprimand.

Before entering the monastery, Sulak had only known people from the upper middle class and the elite. At the temple, he met others from all parts of the very stratified society—beggars and businessmen, prostitutes and princes, fishermen and bankers. With so many different kinds of people coming to visit his teacher, the renowned astrologer, Sulak began to see how Buddhism and Siamese culture were intertwined, and how there was the scriptural Buddhism of the learned on the one hand, and the popular Buddhism of the masses on the other. He

Sulak (*center*), his half-brother, Pravit (*left*), and his cousin Sakol (*right*), when they were monks at Wat Thongnopphakhun in 1944.

understood that popular Buddhism was often mixed with superstitions and animistic beliefs, as he'd observed in the opium dens.

Phra Bhaddramuni made sure to impress on his student one of the core teachings of Buddhism: that the nature of life is change and impermanence. The monks are frequently reminded that death can come at any moment; thus, to practice the Dhamma is an urgent matter. While some monks contemplated death with a pile of human bones actually stacked in front of them, Phra Bhaddramuni chose to etch into Sulak's character the truth of mortality through an even more visceral method. He directed Sulak to construct cremation coffins for the recently deceased who were brought to the temple to be cremated. With the corpse lying before him, Sulak measured the body and built simple coffins with hammer and nails. The smell of death, so pungent in Bangkok's heat, remained in Sulak's nostrils for days—and the remembrance of death in his mind for much longer.

"Phra Bhaddramuni was the most important man in my life, next to my father," Sulak says. "He introduced me to Buddhism and Siamese culture. Without him I'd be like any other Thai, influenced by mainstream education, fashion, and Americanization. He set me deep into my own culture."

Yet Sulak did not idolize his teacher. In living on close terms with Phra Bhaddramuni, he saw all aspects of the man, both his strengths and his weaknesses. He saw how his teacher generously gave away any and all possessions. He also saw how quickly Phra Bhaddramuni could become perturbed, especially when his severe migraines prevented him from leaving his bed, which led to depression.

"I saw all of his negative mood swings, alongside his brilliant scholarship. I watched him benefit so many people, while at the same time being a bit too harsh with some of my fellow novices. What I saw was simply a man. But it was a man who only showed me love."

Phra Bhaddramuni did not teach Sulak meditation. His training was in the scholarly tradition of textual studies, and he had not cultivated deep meditation as a practice. But Sulak was fascinated by the books on meditation he found on his teacher's shelves, with their descriptions of miraculous powers that could be gained from single-pointed concentration, including clairvoyance and even omniscience. One day, Sulak met Luang Anat, an accomplished meditator near his temple. A former naval officer, he had trained with some of Thailand's forest monks. Luang Anat agreed to Sulak's request to study meditation with him. In the evenings Sulak would walk to Luang Anat's home to receive the teachings. He was taught different methods of concentrating the mind, including single-pointed visualization of the Buddha's image in various sizes, some minuscule and others as large as the universe. Luang Anat told Sulak that powers like clairvoyance, and even the ability to walk through walls, were inconsequential side effects of perfecting the practice.

"I was more interested in supernatural powers, but I didn't dedicate enough time to the practice to attain them," Sulak admits, adding, "I didn't really establish a proper meditation practice in my youth."

After Sulak's nearly two years under the tutelage of Phra Bhaddramuni, his father wanted him to come home and return to high school. He feared that if Sulak remained in the monastery, he would fall behind in his studies. He wanted his son to study at his alma mater, a private Catholic school called Assumption College. Sulak reluctantly agreed and asked Phra Bhaddramuni for permission to remove his monk's habit and return to the life of a layperson. The teacher brought Sulak into his quarters and, upon releasing him from his novice vows, gave him a ring that Sulak still cherishes as one of his most precious possession. The ring bears three words: *Buddha, Dhamma, Sangha*—Sulak's sole refuge.

Sulak's reentry into high school did not go smoothly, as he clashed immediately with the Brothers of the Catholic order, and he failed his first midterm exams. Whereas at the temple Sulak had been treated as an equal by his teacher, at Assumption College there was a strict hierarchy. "I admired the Catholic Brothers for their devotion to teaching, their honesty, and their chastity. But I felt that their vow of obedience—not to question their superiors at all—was a bit too much."

Soon thereafter, however, Sulak hit his academic stride and especially enjoyed studying comparative religion and reading recently published books on Thai Buddhism by Sijivo Bhikkhu and Phra Vimaldhamma, the first Chancellor of Chulalongkorn University. Both authors wrote about Buddhism in a modern way—not about meditation, but about ethics, which deepened Sulak's sense of pride in his Buddhist heritage. His pride in the monarchy, as well, was bolstered by his reading of biographies. Sulak recalls, "The market was lush with books, but their range of subjects was narrowly defined—most were either hagiographies of the ruling elite, of kings and princes, or exaltations of the absolute epoch. They blamed the woes that society was experiencing on the 1932 revolutionaries, meaning, by and large, Pridi."

The Catholic priests at Assumption, especially Brother François Hilaire, for whom Sulak developed a deep respect, were of the conservative bent. Brother Hilaire exposed Sulak to the eighteenth-century philosopher and statesman Edmund Burke, the founder of modern British conservatism. In his most famous work, Burke wrote fervently against the French Revolution for having stripped the king, nobility, and church of power and property. Burke saw little virtue in the revolutionary motto, *liberté, égalité, fraternité*, and the Brothers agreed. Sulak dove into the Irishman's works and came to appreciate Burke's endorsement of a rigid class-based society. Although Sulak had liked the way he had been treated as an equal in the monastery, he returned to a conservative attitude that believed society should have defined social classes that supported "Nation, Religion, and Monarchy," rather than any calls for revolution.

Sulak's father died less than a year after Sulak's return to school. The loss crushed Sulak emotionally, but he was comforted by remembering all that his father had given him. "He taught me that I should be independent. I should not yield to any authority or tradition if I didn't find it helpful." In his Thai-language memoir, Sulak reflected that, because he acquired some of his father's stubborn traits, "We might have clashed when I got older"—a comment that ironically describes exactly what happened thirty years later when Sulak became estranged from his own son.

The family's financial situation changed drastically following the father's death. Although they were not rich, Chalerm had been sufficiently well paid in his position at the tobacco company to support the family. After paying for all of the funeral rites, the family had little money left. Sulak's stepmother was hospitalized for a nervous breakdown. Sulak went to live with his mother some hundred miles from Bangkok in a rural village, but the relationship was strained because they argued so often. Sulak admits that he was too judgmental of his mother's animistic beliefs and her customs of wearing amulets and making offerings to spirit houses. "Had I inquired about my mother's beliefs, I would have learned much about Thai culture early on," Sulak said. "But I had no time for superstition and shamanism at that time." Sulak says that he had adopted strong puritanical Buddhist beliefs from his time at the monastery and stubbornly stuck to his own ideas without trying to understand others' beliefs. His judgmentalism about his mother and the harsh way that he criticized her remain one of his life's great regrets.

Because he did not get on well with his mother, Sulak returned to

Bangkok, where he reentered Assumption College to finish high school. Money was short, so part of his father's home was converted into a youth hostel for students at a nearby science college. When Sulak came home from his day at school, he debated endlessly with the boarders in the leafy courtyard, often defending Buddhism and traditional culture against the students who promoted modernism and the superiority of Western science. A number of political topics were also hotly debated following the end of World War II in 1945. The disgraced Phibun fell from power and was charged with war crimes; Pridi became Thailand's democratically elected prime minister; and Thailand was forced to return territory seized from Cambodia, Malaysia, and Laos.

Only a few months before Pridi became the prime minster in 1946, the young King Ananda Mahidhol, who had been living an idyllic life in Switzerland with his mother and younger brother, returned to his homeland. The smiling faces of Ananda and his younger brother by two years, Prince Bhumibol, appeared regularly in the Western and Thai newspapers. The royal family had lived in Switzerland since the 1932 revolution. Sulak recalls the optimism felt throughout the country with the return of the dashing twenty-year-old king. However, six months after his return, a mysterious tragedy struck the royal palace when the young monarch was killed by a single bullet from a Colt .45. The queen mother and others came running and found King Ananda dead in his bedchamber from a shot fired at close range. The last person to have seen the king alive was Prince Bhumibol, who said he had looked in on his brother and found him dozing.

How and why was the king shot? Palace officials struggled to provide the public and diplomats with a credible narrative. Paul Handley, author of an exhaustive biography of King Bhumibol, *The King Never*

Smiles—a book that was banned by the Thai government immediately upon publication in 2006—writes, "Two of the possible explanations considered at the time were simple and understandable. Ananda killed himself, either accidentally while playing with the gun, or deliberately; or Bhumibol, in play, accidentally shot him. Both were feasible, because Ananda and Bhumibol kept loaded guns immediately handy by their beds." Handley dismisses the nefarious third theory of assassination for political reasons. He notes, "Most foreign missions concluded that either Ananda killed himself or Bhumibol did it accidentally."

Initially the palace suggested assassination, but the official explanation was given that the King accidentally shot himself. In the absence of a thorough investigation, gossip and innuendo spread quickly. Andrew Marshall wrote, in his banned book *A Kingdom in Crisis* (2014), that Kukrit and Seni Pramoj, and other members of the royalist bloc, spread unfounded rumors that Pridi was behind a plot to murder the King. The Pramoj brothers were even said to have paid someone to shout in a cinema: "Pridi killed the King!" These rumors were widely believed in the chaos that followed Ananda's death.

With the nation in shock, Prince Bhumibol ascended to the throne as politicians, the aristocracy, and those in the royal court jockeyed to benefit their own positions in the changing political and royal landscape. Handley writes, "Suddenly, life changed prodigiously for Bhumibol. Within hours, the bright, often smiling and joking prince, more interested in European cars and American jazz than anything Thailand had to offer, would be named king of a country in which he had spent less than 5 of his 18 years. He would almost never be seen smiling in public again."

The person who experienced the greatest political blow from the death of King Ananda was none other than Pridi. His opponent Kukrit

Pramoj, a prominent royalist and journalist, smeared Pridi by publishing accusations of regicide in his influential newspaper, *Siam Rath*. Within a year, a coup d'état forced Pridi into exile. Pridi secretly returned and attempted a countercoup in 1949, but he failed and was permanently banished. He spent his exile in China for over twenty years, and then in France. Pridi, the hero of democracy in Thailand, never returned to his homeland.

Sulak, like the majority of his fellow citizens, was distressed about what happened to King Ananda. He had heard disparaging words about Pridi from his father, his Buddhist teacher, and his Catholic schoolteachers, all of whom were ardent royalists. They parroted the journalists' sensationalist charges against Pridi, although there was never any evidence of his involvement in the death. At the time, Sulak believed that Pridi's banishment confirmed his guilt. More than ever, Sulak was convinced that a strong monarch—not a democrat—was what the country needed.

Three men were eventually executed for conspiring to kill the King, but most people believed they were innocent scapegoats. Handley writes, "To this day, despite the tragic effect it had on the lives of so many, the answer remains a mystery. More than any other person concerned, Bhumibol prefers to leave it so. The death opened political fault lines and triggered years of Ayutthayan intrigue. And as it placed the palace at the center of politics, Ananda's death perversely raised the monarchy's profile and, eventually, vastly increased its power."

Decades later, Sulak changed his view of what caused the death of King Ananda. In 2011, Sulak told a reporter for the Canadian newspaper *The Star*, "The truth is the present king killed his brother—accidentally." It is a statement no newspaper in Thailand has ever been willing to print for fear of lèse-majesté.

....

Phra Bhaddramuni blessing Sulak at his home before he leaves for the United Kingdom.

Chapter 2

Saltwater Education

During his education at Assumption College, Sulak proved to be an outstanding student, and a controversial one. For the school magazine that he founded, called *Under the Locust Tree*, he wrote articles daring to criticize prominent government ministers who had disparaged his hero Prince Damrong, as well as some of his own teachers for their way of teaching that included rote learning. He dreamed of becoming a celebrated writer like Phya Anuman, a royalist and a scholar of encyclopedic knowledge who became a mentor to Sulak. Brother Hilaire supported Sulak in his writing but warned him, "Be careful. You are smart, but you are not mindful of the consequences of your words, and that will be your downfall."

Sulak graduated from Assumption College in 1952 at age nineteen. He considered attending Chulalongkorn University in Bangkok, but his mother urged him to receive his higher education in England and even offered to pay for it, as she had recently come into an inheritance.

The Thai elite—whom both Sulak and his mother wished to emulate—believed that to advance themselves in business and politics a "saltwater education" abroad was preferable to a "freshwater schooling" at home.

Sulak immediately conferred with Phra Bhaddramuni. After consulting his astrological texts, Phra Bhaddramuni supported the decision to study in England. Before leaving, Sulak was blessed with a traditional ceremony in which his teacher tied a white benediction cord around his wrist and sprinkled blessed water on his head for protection, while chanting verses to the Buddha. He also presented Sulak with a treasured antique statue of the Buddha consecrated by a famous monk known as Somdet To.

"I was touched. I have worn that amulet that he gave me ever since, and I put it on a chain that my dear mother gave me. Without these people, my teacher and mother, I would have never had the chance to advance my education as I did. And it was my father who taught me to believe in myself."

Sulak's parents and his teacher would have been extremely pleased with the self-assuredness that Sulak brought with him to England in June of 1953. The trip from Bangkok to London took three days, with multiple flights and stops en route in Calcutta, Karachi, Athens, Rome, and Geneva. He strode through the city streets in his newly tailored suit with a cosmopolitan air, as if this were his debut as Thailand's future prime minister—an achievement that Sulak admits he aspired to at the time. As the plane touched down in London, there was no other place in the world he would have rather been, because the United Kingdom was in full celebration of the coronation of their new queen, Elizabeth II. Monarchists are drawn to each other, even across borders, with an unspoken gesture of mutual respect, and Sulak played his role in perpetuating the belief in the superiority of blue blood. The next five years of studying in the UK further molded Sulak's monarchism and an elitist attitude.

Soon after his arrival in London, Sulak called on a senior Thai statesman who had been a friend of his father's. Direk Jayanama, who was Pridi's close associate, had held a number of posts, including Ambassador to the Court of St. James's and Minister of Foreign Affairs. Sulak also telephoned and wrote letters to a handful of other friends or acquaintances living in England at the time and traveled to meet them before he settled into his studies. Building alliances and networks through direct and regular contacts was a personal trait that Sulak cultivated in England and has maintained throughout his life.

The Thai elite who went to England—all ardent royalists—generally attended Oxford or Cambridge. Sulak did not perform well enough on his entrance exams to apply to either; his English-language results were especially disappointing. This failure was a blow to his inflated young ego. The University of Wales, Lampeter, one of the oldest institutions of higher education in the UK, admitted him because of his excellent score in other subjects.

Sulak journeyed by rail from London to Cardiff. As he looked out the train window at the Cambrian Mountains, he thought of the princes and princesses, and the sons of aristocrats, attending Oxford and Cambridge. He still wanted to be there. But he consoled himself by thinking that it would be better to excel at a smaller school than be merely one of many in the Oxbridge crowds. Sulak developed coping strategies such as this early in his life to deal with feelings of inferiority that stemmed from his commoner upbringing in the rigidly stratified society of Thailand. He never indulged in emotional catharsis by revealing his disappointments to friends, whether in England or at home, for that might expose his vulnerabilities. Sulak wanted to project the gravitas of towering public figures extolled by the world he was now entering—men such as Churchill, Eden, de Gaulle, and Franklin Roosevelt.

As it turned out, Sulak was able to embrace his new school with gusto. Lampeter was an extremely strict, cloistered, all-male Anglican institution where daily prayers were offered for the Queen. There he was at home among fellow monarchists. Sulak met his moral tutor, Frank Richard Newte, a reserved English gentleman who not only advised his Siamese pupil on academics, but taught Sulak chess over tea and took him on long walks into the Wales countryside and along the Teifi and Dulas rivers. Tutor Newte guided Sulak toward a Bachelor of Arts degree, which included studies of Greek, ancient history, British and European history, English literature, and philosophy.

Perhaps the greatest influence Tutor Newte had on Sulak was to deepen his belief in the primacy of a monarch and the necessary role of the aristocracy in leading the masses, because it was they who wielded the keenest judgment and most refined intellect. "The British empire was successful because of the aristocrats. And the more we've been influenced by democracy in this country, the more we have been ruined," Tutor Newte told Sulak, who nodded with approval. Sulak agreed with Newte that his own country should be run not by the plebs—common citizens— but rather by the likes of a king, or royalty like Prince Damrong, and high-standing aristocrats.

Sulak has continued to believe that his study of the Greeks was a correct guide for the way his home country should be ruled. "My reading of Plato, Socrates, and Aristotle still influences me," he says. "They said the best ruler was a monarch, a good king. Of course, an evil king can turn into tyranny. The second best option is rule by the aristocracy, but if that goes sideways it becomes a terrible plutocracy. And the least favorable form of rule is democracy because of the lack of qualified people in

Sulak Sivaraksa and the Path of Socially Engaged Buddhism

positions of power. Just look at all the third-rate people who are elected to high office in the US, the UK, and everywhere."

Even in later years, when Sulak saw merit in democracy, he never fully embraced it as the ideal form of governance because of his own deeply ingrained royalism and Tutor Newte's influence. In Sulak's collection of essays on Pridi Banomyong, *Powers That Be* (English edition, 1999), he reflected on this influence: "My English tutor at the university unrelentingly dumbed me down, adamantly exaggerating the merits of aristocracy. He insisted that Britain became a great power because of the brilliance of its ruling elites, its aristocrats. British aristocrats, he maintained, were impeccably schooled in the just and fair administration of the state. There was no room for the three shibboleths from the French Revolution—liberty, equality, and fraternity. . . . I myself was taught to idolize the conservative Churchill and Eden, and therefore my tutor's logic forcefully swayed me."

Sulak not only adopted Western ways of thinking but also fully embraced English manners, even sporting the cane and cap of a country gentleman. At the same time, his reverence for his Siamese roots was deepening. Writing articles about Thailand for university publications, as well as sending cross-cultural reportage back home to be published in various journals, Sulak used his skill as a communicator across boundaries of creed, nationalism, and political allegiance. He tried to find the most appropriate modes of cultural expression as a means to dig deeper into who he was, and who he wanted to become.

His university compelled all of its 130 students to attend chapel three mornings and three evenings per week. In view of his Buddhist faith, Sulak was excused from the Christian services, but he chose to attend. Sulak enjoyed the singing of Christian hymns and the camaraderie with classmates, and also used these activities as ways to improve his

English. But though he was a quick study when it came to social etiquette and religious customs, he did not focus as much effort on mastering the necessary knowledge for his academic studies. He had enthusiasm for contemplating and debating Western philosophy with his tutor and classmates, but he used these activities to bolster his own monarchist views rather than to improve his performance on essays and exams. Sulak loved to don a black gown for the daily formal dinner at the high table—though he prayed to the Buddha during grace. He wore his tweed jacket to the local pub and debated world politics with his fellow students. He tried to lecture his classmates about the virtues of Buddhism, without arousing much interest. With all this activity, however, he did not produce academically and failed his first-year exams.

"The English I was with were dreadfully against the French, and would say the French study too much, become too intellectual, and eventually turn into Communists." Sulak said his fellow students told him, "'We in England don't study that much! We go to lectures in the morning, though really we just drink tea, and in the afternoon we play cricket. If you are English and an aristocrat, you don't let others see that you are studying hard!' This is why I flunked my first year, I didn't study at all."

Sulak had never failed so publicly at anything before. "It hurt me so much, and I felt bad," he admits. Kapilavaddho, the first Englishman to be ordained a monk in Thailand, was in the UK at the time (1955), founding the English Sangha Trust, and he consoled Sulak, who afterward meditated. "The Dhamma did help me at this time," he said.

Sulak felt that he would be stigmatized if he repeated the studies he had failed, so he wanted to take leave from Lampeter, to refocus and to study law in London—after all, he did aspire to become prime minister, and a barrister's training would be of use. Tutor Newte supported his decision, and Sulak was soon accepted to study at the Middle Temple in London. It was this decision to study law that gave Sulak even more tools of the precise argumentation and critical analysis that became hallmarks of his character.

Sulak stayed on in London after his first year's pursuit of a law degree. He also resumed his education in Wales, traveling back and forth from his studio flat in London to the stone walls of Lampeter to study philosophy, especially Descartes, Spinoza, and Locke. He took the summers for extended trips to France and Switzerland to continue his study of French, as well as visiting every corner of the United Kingdom, networking with fellow Thai students, and taking part in the Thai Students Association of England. He gained academic degrees in philosophy, English, and history from Lampeter after three years, but he had yet to complete his law examinations.

Sulak continued his study of law in London. His time there brought him into contact with scholars and students of Buddhism and Southeast Asian studies at the University of London's School of Oriental and African Studies (SOAS). He also joined the Pali Text Society as well as the Buddhist Society, working with its founder, Christmas Humphreys. It was Humphreys who sparked Sulak's critical thinking about Buddhism's role in society. He had warned Sulak that the primary responsibility of a spiritual practitioner was to meditate, not to become involved with political affairs. "This is where the Catholic Church went wrong," Humphreys told Sulak. "They should have never got involved with the social welfare." Sulak respectfully disagreed.

"I felt strange because in my understanding, meditation was of course important. But for a lay Buddhist, in my tradition you have to start with generosity, and then a moral and ethical code, and this is how we can be active in society, how not to exploit, and how to promote justice."

At the time, Sulak did not have the experience or know-how to actualize the ways Buddhism ought to work in society for positive social change. He knew the philosophy but not the application. It was only a couple of decades later, in the 1970s, that Sulak formulated a vision for renewing society through socially engaged Buddhism, saying, "If Buddhists only want to meditate and are not interested in social change, then this is not Buddhism but escapism."

After five years in England, Sulak decided to return to Thailand in 1958 to see his mother and Phra Bhaddramuni. Although he had not yet sat for the bar and had to take a leave of absence from the Thai section of BBC radio, he nonetheless felt a need to reconnect with his family and homeland.

Sulak had not realized the massive changes that had taken place in Thailand during his few years of absence. The country had become central to the developing geopolitical struggle in the region. Following World War II, the United States had identified Thailand as a critical location for halting the spread of Communism. America's attention brought not only a massive military buildup, but also money for new roads and airports, power plants, and construction projects on an unprecedented scale. Upon arriving in Bangkok, Sulak passed by the new harbor that had been built in Bangkok about five miles from his home. The new harbor caused saltwater to flow up the river and had destroyed the orchards he used to roam in his childhood. Where mango, lychee, and durian trees had once flourished beside the ancient canals, now Sulak saw only roads stretching from the harbor to the center of the city.

Despite the shocking changes in the city, and witnessing America's emerging political and military influence in his country, Sulak enjoyed his return and reuniting with his mother and venerated teacher.

Parties were thrown at Assumption College for Sulak, their first graduate to return from the UK with a degree. The Thai Ministry of Education recruited him for work, and Shell Oil offered very lucrative employment as a junior executive. Sulak declined these offers. His heart was still in England, which provided a rich intellectual landscape, not to mention the opportunity to continue his law studies and his work for the BBC. His mother urged, "Just take a good, secure job here." Phra Bhaddramuni, after consulting his astrological charts, suggested that it would be more fruitful for Sulak to return to England. Perhaps there was something in the palm leaves that told him Sulak needed to finish what he had begun abroad before he would make his mark in Thailand.

Sulak returned to London and his job at the BBC in the winter of 1958 and moved into a one-bedroom flat with a simple stove, and a communal water cabinet down the hall. Sulak excelled on BBC radio and was given free rein to file whatever reports he wished. He traveled throughout England, producing stories of interest for listeners back home, which brought him name recognition in Thailand as an up-and-coming intellectual. He also gained membership, through the personal connections he had made at The Middle Temple and the Inns of Court, and in some of the exclusive clubs in London. Sulak made it a point to attend high tea at the clubs when the Queen or other English royalty was present. He also continued his personal study of Pali and Buddhism, and helped to organize events for the only Theravada Buddhist Temple in the UK, the Buddhist Vihara. Every day brought new opportunities that Sulak seized with enthusiasm.

After less than a year of operation, in 1959 the BBC decided to close its Thai section. Sulak had learned to meet disappointment with a shrug of the shoulder and his common refrain: "Never mind. Move on."

He would not let himself dwell for too long on matters beyond his control. Sulak spoke to friends who helped him find work teaching Thai at the SOAS.

When it was announced that the King and Queen of Thailand would make a royal visit to England and the Continent in 1960, the BBC in London reopened its Thai section and asked Sulak to return as its principal correspondent. Not only was he skilled in the technical aspects of radio reporting, but he was thoroughly acquainted with Chakri court etiquette, including the rarefied language reserved solely for addressing the monarch.

This was the first state visit to the United Kingdom by King Bhumibol. Military rulers had long kept the thirty-three-year old king tightly controlled. But after yet another coup in 1957 that had brought General Sarit Thanarat to power in Bangkok, restrictions on King Bhumibol had been relaxed and he was allowed to travel internationally. The best-known journalist in Thailand, Kukrit Pramoj, who worked as a liaison between the palace and the BBC, oversaw Sulak's reporting of the royal visit. Kukrit, some twenty years Sulak's senior, was a minor royal and a prolific writer of all genres, including poetry. Sulak admired Kukrit greatly at this time and had read all his works, from his daily columns in Thailand's popular newspaper, *Siam Rath*, to his novels, such as *The Four Reigns*, and many works of nonfiction. *A King of Siam Speaks* (1948) was coauthored by Kukrit and his brother Seni as a protest against *Anna and*

Previous page, top: (*right*) with Thai and English friends in the United Kingdom in 1953.

Previous page, bottom: Sulak (*right*) and his colleagues at the British Broadcasting Corporation (BBC) Thai Section in 1959.

the *King of Siam*, Margaret Landon's 1944 novel (and the 1946 dramatic film made from it), for its offensive, distorted portrait of King Mongkut, Rama IV. (The same Landon work later inspired a 1951 stage musical and a 1956 film musical under the title *The King and I*.) Kukrit was a giant in Thailand's popular culture, and had even starred in *The Ugly American*, in which he acted alongside Marlon Brando, playing the role of the prime minister of a fictional Southeast Asian country. He was said to have used his connections for financial and political gain like no other individual in Thailand. As a politician, he would later serve as Thailand's prime minister (1975–1976). During the royal visit, Sulak shadowed this towering figure and at the same time filed his own stories.

Sulak felt truly in his element when mingling with ultraroyalists, including both Thai and English aristocrats, and reporting from Buckingham Palace, Guildhall, and other chambers where the strictest protocol was followed. On a few occasions Sulak even spoke to King Bhumibol himself, and was proud to display his command of royal turns of phrase that very few Thai knew. He continued to cover every move of the royal couple, traveling with the press corps to the Netherlands. After the King and Queen's visit, Sulak received a handwritten note from the King's private secretary, praising his journalism and thanking him for a poem that he wrote in honor of the royal visit. Sulak had thus been a notable contributor to the success of the international coming-out party, shining the best light on the Buddhist monarchy with his reporting on all the virtues of his King. "My participation in the royal visit was a high point for me in my time in London," Sulak says.

Nevertheless, Kukrit watched over Sulak with a wary eye on the young upstart's confident demeanor. On several occasions he reprimanded Sulak with offhand reminders that no matter how hard he might try, he

Sulak Sivaraksa and the Path of Socially Engaged Buddhism

King Bhumibol and Queen Sirikit at the garden of
the Royal Thai Embrassy in London, in 1961, and Kukrit
Pramoj (*center, with eyeglasses*), and Sulak (*right*).

would remain a pleb, one of the many whom the King and aristocrats like
Kukrit were endowed to rule over. Sulak did not appreciate Kukrit's
comments, but they could not diminish his deeply ingrained royalism
and unquestioning loyalty to the aristocracy. Sulak took Kukrit's attitude
in stride and carried on with his job.

Following the excitement of the royal visit, Sulak returned to
studying law. He was only twenty-nine years old but had already gained
some prominence in London. Regarded as an expert on Thai affairs by the
English media and on Siamese Buddhism by academics, he was sought out
for interviews and invited to lecture at Oxford, Cambridge, and SOAS. Life
was comfortable in England, and with a military dictator still in control
back home, Sulak had little interest in returning. Because the Thai political

environment was so stifling to intellectual creativity, he considered remaining indefinitely in England.

One evening on the SOAS campus, Sulak met a man from Burma who taught at the university. He had noticed that the Burmese were quite distinct from the Siamese in one important respect: "We like to adapt ourselves to our surroundings, to act like Englishmen when we're in English company—drinking beer, going to the pub, smoking a pipe. But the Burmese were entirely different. For however long they lived in London, they dressed in the Burmese style; they did not go to the pubs, and during the Buddhist Rain Retreat period, they ate only one or two strictly vegetarian meals a day. They were very serious. I admired them."

The Burmese man asked Sulak, "When will you go home?"

"I don't know. I like it here. Perhaps I won't go home," Sulak told him.

"Mr. Sulak, if you can go home, you *should* go home. You should give yourself a chance to do something for your country. People with your background and education are not many. As for me, I can't go home. Since the military took over, my country has been going to the dogs. They would not let me go back. If I'd had a chance, I would have gone back. I have been nostalgic about my country all my life. Don't follow my bad example."

Then and there, Sulak realized that he must go home. But he had to get that law degree first! He crammed for the exam and sat for the bar successfully in 1961. Having decided to leave, and thinking he might never return, Sulak embarked on one last trip across Europe—the Netherlands, Germany, France, Italy, and Greece—staying with Thai diplomats, princes, and Buddhist friends.

While he was in Bonn staying with the Thai ambassador, Direk Jayanama, the news came that Phra Bhaddramuni had died, having hanged himself. Jayanama, too, was devoted to Bhaddramuni, and both men were shocked. Sulak decided to return immediately, to be able to pay his respects before the cremation.

En route home, Sulak penned a biography in which he praised Phra Bhaddramuni's erudition and other talents. Although he was aware of his teacher's less admirable traits and had never idealized him, for once in his writing Sulak restrained his customary censorious tone. Had he chosen to criticize his teacher, he could have noted that suicide is a violation of the first Buddhist precept for both monks and laypeople to refrain from killing (*ahimsa*, nonharming). But Sulak would not pass judgment. Indeed, he was deeply pained to think of the mental torment that his teacher must have gone through, to commit such an act of despair. Sulak remembered the anguish he saw in his own father, who suffered more from the fear of death than from the cancer that ended his life. Knowing that Phra Bhaddramuni also endured great anguish before dying weighed heavily on Sulak.

This was the man Sulak respectfully regarded as his true teacher. All others from whom he had learned—from the Brothers of Assumption College to Tutor Newte and the professors at the Middle Temple—had been but spiritual friends along the path. But now his only teacher was gone. As he witnessed the corpse being prepared for cremation, Sulak reflected, "If I had been in the country, maybe my teacher wouldn't have committed suicide. Nobody challenged him or talked straight to him except me."

....

Chapter 3

Intellectual Gadfly

Sulak returned home in 1962, after a total of eight years in the United Kingdom. The social and political climate was steeped in Cold War fear. The Communist threats from just beyond their borders made the Thai anxious. They were also afraid of their own military dictator, Field Marshal Sarit Thanarat. Sarit had consolidated power in 1958 after pushing Phibun into exile. Key to Sarit's rise was the cooperation of King Bhumibol, who had sided with him in his power struggle with Phibun. Once again, Thailand was under the control of a military strongman. The difference this time was that King Bhumibol had endorsed it.

Sulak watched Sarit use the three pillars of "Thai-ness"—Nation,

Previous page, top: Sulak meeting King Bhumibol at the Grand Palace in Bangkok on the occasion of the Asian Writers Conference in 1964.

Previous page, bottom: The office of the *Social Science Review* in 1965.

Religion, and Monarchy—to bolster his authoritarian rule. Aided by US propaganda and financing, Sarit had revived the monarchy after its near-eclipse in 1932. Sarit and his military men and their US patrons wanted King Bhumibol to be a focus of unity and stability, while still remaining under their control. King Bhumibol welcomed the platform Sarit provided to expand his royal role at home and abroad. Sarit linked the monarchy to the army by inventing elaborate rituals, such as having the troops pledge allegiance to the throne and flag, and arranging for the King and Queen to accept honorary military command positions. Sarit revived other Buddhist ceremonies that empowered the monarchy with divine-like qualities, some of which had been done away with in 1932, such as royal presentation of monastic robes to the monks, and offering ceremonial fans emblazoned with the King's insignia. Sarit also amended the laws governing the sangha to further bring the Buddhist ecclesiastical hierarchy under political control.

Sarit brought a period of extreme brutal rule—even more repressive than the Phibun era. Baker and Phongpaichit note how, after meeting with President Eisenhower and Secretary of State Dulles in Washington in 1958, Sarit returned to Thailand to carry out the coup that pushed out Phibun, and "declared martial law, annulled parliament, discarded the constitution, banned political parties, and arrested hundreds of politicians, journalists, intellectuals, and activists. The US cheered and granted US $20 million in economic aid." Sulak described Sarit as "the worst tyrant we have ever had."

The United States formed a strong alliance with Sarit, as it had with previous dictators in Thailand, to combat Communist movements in Southeast Asia. For Sarit and his successor, General Thanom Kittikachorn, who ruled until 1973, also by dictate and marshal law, America provided protection from the external threat of Communists in

Sulak Sivaraksa and the Path of Socially Engaged Buddhism

Vietnam, Laos, and Cambodia, and the training and weapons to quell any indigenous uprisings. Sarit promised to keep Thailand free of Communist infiltration from outside and to root out insurgents from the Communist Party of Thailand (CPT) who were based in the jungles of the northern and northeastern frontier. Thailand was a mainstay of anti-Communism for the United States in a region fraught with political insecurity. President Truman had declared that Thailand would be the bulwark against Communist expansion in the region. President Kennedy's administration followed suit, highlighted Thailand's neighbor Laos as the most tenuous security challenge in the world, and sent hundreds of military and covert advisers to Thailand. But it was Presidents Johnson and Nixon who ordered the ground forces and established large US Air Force bases in Thailand, which became the most important country to prosecute their war in Vietnam. By the mid-1960s, almost 80 percent of US Air Force targets in North Vietnam were flown out of bases in Thailand, including Operation Rolling Thunder. And, at the peak of the war in 1969, more US airmen were serving in Thailand than in South Vietnam.

The Vietnam War brought American culture to Thailand. Historically it was the highly educated elite, mostly from Bangkok, who were exposed to European and American culture, mainly from traveling abroad. Now America was on Sulak's home turf. The United States expanded its influence through its support of education, transportation, construction, and industrial agriculture, and through a steady proliferation of US servicemen. American culture inundated Thailand. The tourism industry also started to develop at this time, beginning with large hotels in Bangkok, Chiang Mai, and eventually the southern beach resorts. The "American Strips" on New Phetchaburi Road, not far from Sulak's home, flourished with new nightclubs, bars, brothels, and massage parlors for the tourists and military servicemen. Sulak was astonished by the rapid increase in vehicles and taxis, the construction of drab high-rise buildings, and the destruction of the natural environment in and around Bangkok.

Thailand's economy grew rapidly with US investment. Ancient gilded pagodas and Buddhist temples around the city were now in the shadows of new concrete office buildings. Highways were bulldozed through the jungle and tessellated paddy fields, expanding Bangkok's city perimeter and connecting towns in the north of the country. All the economic development and construction in Bangkok needed a labor force. The landless poor who couldn't find work as rubber packers or in the feed mills or tobacco-curing yards in the north and northeast of the country migrated to Bangkok for jobs, swelling the capital's population. Sulak remembered when longboats along the canals were the primary means of transportation and commerce; he would tell his friends in London that Bangkok was the "Venice of the East." His own teak house in the center of Bangkok was rapidly becoming an anomaly as traditional wooden homes were pulled down and the land was sold to real estate developers. By the end of the 1960s, Bangkok had doubled in size in less than a decade, to three million residents. A polluted and homogenized city emerged before Sulak's eyes.

Sulak saw few positive elements in the American influence in Thailand. His critical views sharpened in his writing, though he was not offering solutions. As he wrote in a collection of his writings in English, *Siam Through a Looking Glass* (1973):

> American experts penetrated within many Thai Government agencies, even in provinces, and we developed our country in the American image in most respects. Our educators and administrators, our soldiers and policemen, were trained en

Sulak Sivaraksa and the Path of Socially Engaged Buddhism

bloc in America or by Americans. Our officials were even trained to suppress our own people! Development means more roads upcountry, which means that the rich can buy more land in the distant provinces. Development means officials have more access to the people in the rural areas, which means more dissatisfaction with officialdom. Without Parliament and or the free press, there was no real leadership developed in the open. . . . In the towns, the US presence had had catastrophic effects on Thai culture. The Thai elite became greedy and corrupted. The best way to earn money was through working with the Americans, who had a lot of money they did not have to account for. The rich and the powerful got the bigger share, from dealings in weapons and heroin, to catering for the Rest and Recreation for soldiers from Vietnam. . . . The poor and the beautiful could also earn something through manual work and sex. As a result, we are now known for our prostitutes, cheating and corruption. . . . How will this benefit us, I do not know. And to be fair, we should not blame all this on the Americans. But without American presence to the extent already indicated, would all this have been possible?

Sulak was determined to find ways to contribute to society that might guide the country in a direction different from that in which Sarit and the other militants were steering. But he wasn't going to work just anywhere; he was adamant about maintaining his independence. The character molded by his father and Buddhist teacher was manifesting in his refusal of the employment offered in the civil service and government, by the Southeast Asia Treaty Organization (SEATO), and by American and British companies. He felt he would merely have been contributing to the negative direction of his country. The dictator Sarit even offered Sulak a job as a speechwriter, which would have guaranteed him access to elite circles of power. He refused all the offers. Instead, he began to piece together work that allowed him to contribute his own insights and views to his society, even while remaining outside any institutional control. He was a visiting lecturer in philosophy and ethics at Chulalongkorn, Silpakorn, and Thammasat universities; he translated journals and newspapers from Thai into English for the British Information Service; and he offered English-language tutorials to students preparing to study abroad. He was also reacquainting himself with the intellectual landscape of Thailand, which to his dismay he found lacked innovation or critical outlook.

The dictators and military rulers in Thailand had repressed intellectuals and those with dissenting political views since 1947. Legislation was passed that banned writing "any matter ambiguously defamatory or contemptuous of the Thai government, or any ministry, public body, or department of the government" and "any false matter of a nature tending to panic, worry, or frighten the people or matter tending to incite, or arouse disorder, or conflict with public order or morality, or prophecies concerning the fate of the nation which might upset people." Sulak knew many individuals who had been jailed, disappeared, silenced, or even executed for their contrarian views, or accused of being Communists. By the time Sulak returned to Thailand in the early 1960s, even academics and professors dared not teach or write anything of a sensitive nature because the universities were controlled by the military and had placed their generals as the rectors. Student clubs were banned throughout the nation. The intellectual tools that Sulak had honed in the UK—writing, debate, logic, reason, and wit—if wielded in Thailand would land him in prison, or worse. "The dictatorship had created darkness," Sulak wrote in *Siam Through a Looking Glass*. He wanted to find some way to crack the system and let the light in.

There was a small group of intellectuals in Thailand. They were not members of an avant-garde but instead traditional royalists who wrote about Siamese arts, literature, poetry, and history, promoting their conservative views of a proper Thai way of life. These individuals congregated at elegant gatherings in government-endorsed places like the Siam Society, the Buddhist Association of Thailand, and the Thai Royal Academy. A more progressive group, also concerned about improving the lives of their fellow citizens, was made up of members of academia and the government bureaucracy, but their works made scant impact on government leaders. These intellectuals were more consumers of knowledge than experts in any position to change and create policy.

Where did Sulak fall in the spectrum between traditionalists and progressives? Right in the middle. He remained a staunch royalist with a distrust in democracy, an elitist who had the knowledge to validate his views, and a young intellectual with a growing enthusiasm for his own Siamese roots. He was skeptical of international foreign aid, especially from the United States and Japan, who had their own development agenda, but was still willing, when the opportunity arose later, to accept their money to use for his own projects. Importantly, Sulak was powerfully motivated. He held a deep conviction that he knew what was best for his society, as well as a strong disdain for anyone who disagreed with him. Thus, he would not be stopped.

For those intellectuals who wanted to push the envelope by criticizing the government, the military, or any other pillar of power in Thailand—except the monarchy—the only recourse was to do so indirectly, possibly by using humor or by associating their ideas with a prestigious group in society. Sulak rarely opted for humor; it was too slow to change his opponents' minds. Instead, he often linked his own thinking to that of past heroes, ranging from kings to the Buddha himself. This method successfully enabled him to avoid censure and even arrest.

For example, when Sulak lamented the intellectual climate of the 1960s, he connected his views to those of Prince Damrong. In a biographical essay on the prince in *Siam Through a Looking Glass*, he wrote:

> The absence of endogenous Thai intellectual creativity seems to be rather obvious. The prevailing fashion of the day tends to rely more on the transfer of knowledge, especially from abroad, rather than on self-reliant creativity or conservation of the national identity. The country's philosophy is to follow the western capitalist goals of development, economically, socially and culturally. Without popular participation or freedom of expression, the country is bound to stagnate and members of the younger generation lose their respect for their seniors—a group of second- and third-rate hypocrites who are in charge of the country at various levels. They only care for their own wealth and are without any real concern for social justice or the well-being of the multitude, who are exploited more and more by the unjust social system within the country, as well as from abroad. Neither do they plan positively or seriously about the future of the country. Anyone who really cares for society and his own intellectual independence is alienated from the present political system. He is either not allowed to take any part in the development process of his country, or is forced to live abroad or in the jungle—not to mention prison.

Needing to earn a living, Sulak found steady work at the newly established University Press of Thailand, also known as the Social Science Association Press, which was funded by the US government. Sulak's skills as a writer and editor were in demand, and this gave him a way to contribute concretely to society. The Thai education system, including at universities, was almost an entirely oral didactic tradition. Students essentially did not use books but instead sat for lectures. Books were viewed as costly luxuries, not critical to education. As the University of California anthropologist Herbert P. Phillips wrote in *Change and Persistence in Thai Society*, "There are students who have graduated from Thailand's finest university having read no more than four books during their entire undergraduate career." The University Press, of which Sulak was part creator, was charged to improve the standard of textbooks at colleges and universities, and to offer them more affordably.

While the work at the University Press inspired Sulak, it wasn't until he founded the *Social Science Review* (Sangkhomsat Parithat) in 1963 that he realized the full potential of his voice. "It was his love for literature, for writing and publishing, that gave Sulak a platform, and ultimately his voice," social activist Anchalee Kurutach said.

The *Social Science Review* was Thailand's first intellectual journal, modeled after *Encounter* in England and *The Atlantic Monthly* in the United States. There were other progressive writings published at the time, but they were underground and had little distribution. Sulak solicited funding from the Asia Foundation and founded the *Review* under the auspices of the Social Science Association. Although restrictions on establishing new publications were imposed by the military dictatorship, Sulak maneuvered around the authorities with the support of Prince Wan Waithayakorn, who was president of the Social Science Association. Sulak could never have guessed that his six years as the *Review*'s founding editor would become one of the greatest achievements of his life. Not only did the *Review* become the intellectual voice of the nation, promoting a more open and just society in Thailand; it was also instrumental in awakening the awareness among students that eventually led to the overthrow of the military regime in 1973. The impact of the *Review* in Thailand is still evident today (although it ceased publication many years ago), because countless men and women—including senior members of parliament, alternative educators, artists, musicians, and progressive monks and nuns—recall how important the journal was in opening their minds and inspiring change in the 1960s and '70s.

At the time of its founding, Sulak envisioned that the *Review* would stimulate its readers to glean insights from Thailand's great thinkers, writers, poets, and artists of the past, in ways that could inform their present actions. Sulak was no revolutionary; he merely hoped for reforms that would break up the calcified group-think in the Thai consciousness that stifled creativity and independence. His goal was to inspire critical thinking among the highly stratified classes of society— from the King and Queen and other royals and aristocrats, to military generals and politicians—and especially among students and the younger generation. Sulak's life was playing out like that of the protagonist of the country's first best-selling novel, *Lakhon Haeng Chiwat* (Life Is a Play), written shortly before the 1932 coup by Prince Akat Damkoeng: the story of a Thai who travels abroad, gains new perspectives on his own society, then returns to dedicate himself to changing it for the better.

Sulak contacted nearly all the intellectuals in Thailand and asked them to contribute essays, verse, drama, and illustrations for the *Review*. Initially the publication avoided touching on politics, with not even a mention of the Vietnam War. But after the first year, Sulak and other contributors began to publish criticism of their government's policies and politicians. One issue revealed the actual number of US troops residing in the country—at the time, a highly confidential figure in Thailand. It was a very daring move.

Sulak also used the *Review* as a personal platform to launch the attacks against Kukrit Pramoj that were to continue throughout his life. The deference for Kukrit that Sulak had once felt, especially when they worked together in England, had all but dissolved by this time. This might have seemed surprising, since the two men were similar in many ways, as confirmed by longtime Thai diplomat and former Prime Minister Anand Panyarachun. Anand worked closely with Kukrit in the 1970s at the senior most government level and knew him personally. Anand met Sulak in the United Kingdom during university and got to know him well during his two terms as prime minister in the 1990s, when they worked together in poverty alleviation in rural areas in Thailand. Anand observes, "Sulak is very much like Kukrit. They are both geniuses. Very learned about practically everything—arts, poetry, literature, and religion. Both are sharp tongued, and have elements of envy in their character. And that is why they don't get along!"

Kukrit's and Sulak's larger-than-life egos fueled their prolific output as writers and inspired the ever-widening group of young students around them who sought their advice and support. But the two men were different in profound ways. Sulak was an idealist who sought to work for the common good; Kukrit had been deemed a strategic opportunist with no consistent moral or political principles, according to the distinguished historian Prof. Nidhi Eoseewong. Kukrit defended the aristocracy and class-based birthrights; Sulak defended the underdog and supported the marginalized and the poor, especially after 1973, by speaking out on their behalf and advocating for their rights. "I want to be with the oppressed,"

Sulak says, and reminds students often, "It is better to keep distance from the powers that be."

Prof. Nidhi said, "Kukrit was not someone who, like Sulak, could act as either an idealist or a pragmatist, because he was only a pragmatist, doing only those things that practically benefited himself. It is true that Kukrit was seen as the authority on everything in society. But he was a hypocrite because he didn't have any principles that he upheld consistently. He changed his principles according to the situation. And of course Sulak criticized him for that."

Kukrit was feared because of the power implicit in his royal heritage. He spoke down to nearly everyone. The Bangkok political elite accommodated Kukrit, while preferring that Sulak and his critical voice and publications disappear. Kukrit often responded to Sulak's controversial *Review* writings with harsh criticism in his own *Siam Rath* newspaper. The intellectual rivalry between Kukrit and Sulak—carried on mostly in print—spanned forty years, until Kukrit's death in 1995. Prof. Nidhi observed, "All of the effective and influential intellectuals are performers. Kukrit's performance, he was the best. And Sulak is not far behind him. The skill of performance gives you some kind of power in relation with other people . . . just as when you are on stage and can control the situation."

Kukrit's wife, Mrs. Pakpring Thongyai, told Sulak, "You are the only person who ever captured the true spirit of Kukrit in writing"—a reference to Sulak's 1973 essay "M. R. Kukrit Pramoj Whom I Know." But Kukrit did not appreciate the essay. Even though they were far from being friends, Sulak regretted not following his impulse to visit Kukrit during his final illness. "I should have practiced the Dhamma more by going to see him, to reconcile. To be honest, Kukrit was more kind to me than I have been kind to him. But my stance was never so much about him as a

person, as about how he upheld upper-class privilege against the poor."
Emboldened by the intellectual dueling with the likes of Kukrit and others, Sulak began to publish his own and others' views that were increasingly critical of the Thai government and military. Why did the Sarit and Thanom dictatorships allowed the *Review* to print the dissenting voices? Apparently the military leaders felt they had nothing to fear from a small group of Western-educated intellectuals with no political influence. The journal's survival was also likely due to the royal sponsorship by Prince Wan Waithayakorn, at least for the six years when Sulak was editor.

A transformative moment for Sulak occurred in 1966 when the progressive Prince Sitthiporn told him, "Yes, this country needs an intellectual magazine. But don't let it become intellectual masturbation." Sulak believed that he was helping his countrymen with his writings, by recounting the intellectual history of Siam. When he objected to the implication that his journal amounted to just highbrow self-indulgence that was of no benefit to anyone else, the Prince countered, "Do you know anything about farmers? They suffer, and you know nothing about it!"

This exchange sparked a dramatic shift in Sulak's perspective. He was able to see how his top-down approach was arrogant and flawed. Now, instead of presuming to educate the intellectual elites through criticism, he was determined to take meaningful action himself. He began to visit rural villages, temples, and rice fields across Thailand to witness the lives and struggles of the common people. By meeting with farmers, loggers, fishermen, and day laborers, he learned a profound lesson that he reiterates to this day: that to alleviate suffering—whatever its source, such as poverty, war, injustice, or environmental disaster—we must go and be with the people who suffer, experience their hardships at first hand, and try to connect deeply on the ground with the actual situation.

When Sulak traveled among his countrymen and women, he connected with their suffering and believed he saw the causes of both their poverty and their deep mental suffering. At the root of his society's problems, Sulak believed, was a crisis of Siamese identity—individually and collectively as a nation; this had to be addressed if the country was to undergo the renewal it needed. Loss of pride in the Siamese heritage and alienation from traditional cultural, religious, and social values, Sulak felt, had led to this identity crisis, which was exacerbated by a variety of modern influences.

The various iterations of nationalism partially caused the identity crisis because the attempts to unify the people under one national Thai identity had the effect of withering many ethnic and indigenous traditions. This nationalism was promoted at the beginning of the twentieth century—especially during the reign (1910–1925) of Vajiravudh, King Rama VI, and extending through the military dictatorships of the 1960s. After the arrival of the Americans during the Vietnam War, when Western culture and especially capitalism were widely accepted in Thailand, Sulak felt the identity crisis was brought to a critical head. Sulak's intellectual activities of the 1960s were an attempt to increase understanding of this identity crisis, and then to apply a Buddhist approach to renewing society through education and self-reliance. Thai historians have called Sulak's approach "conservative radicalism." Thongchai Winichakul described it in *Siam Mapped: A History of the Geo-Body of a Nation* (1997): "Basically it attacks the failure of modern Thai society in the light of Buddhist Thai tradition, arguing that modernity, capitalism, and consumerism have uprooted Thai people from the fundamentals of Thai civilization—hence the degradation of modern culture and the deterioration of morality and Buddhism in Thai society as a whole."

Sulak wrote in *Siam in Crisis* (1990):

We are so susceptible to the influence of foreign intellectuals that some of us have followed Nietzsche in claiming that God is dead. Thais today scarcely comprehend their religion or cultural heritage. In a recent seminar on educational planning, for example, there was no mention of the relevance of Buddhism to contemporary education or in the role of monks in educating rural villages. . . . This discussion was so bad it was an insult to the monks. If today's intellectuals would only look to the past, they would see how strongly their predecessors felt about the dangers of letting the education of our youth slip out of the hands of the monks. The problem for our generation is how to recombine the pattern of religion, education and culture which are divided into disparate themes in so many foreign lands. We should stop imitating the foreigners and return to the essence in the Thai experience.

In the midst of Sulak's most dynamic period of his life, he had been courting a young lady named Nilchawee Pattanothai. Though Sulak may have been the more outgoing of the two, Nilchawee matched him in self-confidence, according to their friends. Their courtship—filled with activities like lingering over meals at Chinese restaurants, watching flying kites on the promenade next to the Grand Palace in the heart of Bangkok, and going to the cinema—was a period of lightheartedness that Sulak would rarely indulge in again, because of pressure from his work. Sulak asked for her hand in 1964. Prince Dhani Niwat, President of the Privy Council and Siamese historian whom Sulak greatly admired, conducted their wedding ceremony. The couple moved into Sulak's father's home in the Bangrak district of Bangkok, a comfortable traditional pile-raised house, with mango trees in the courtyard. As the marriage progressed, Nilchawee was supportive of Sulak when he made unconventional and

Wedding ceremony of Sulak and Nilchawee at
Prince Dhani Niwat's palace on 27 November 1964.

sometimes dangerous life choices, including those that would affect the whole family. Nilchawee taught home economics at a local college while also managing her household and raising their son and two daughters. She also helped Sulak maintain his nonstop schedule of writing, publishing, and traveling the world, quietly observing his activities and rarely asserting her own political views. The social activist Anchalee Kurutach likened Nilchawee's role to that of the classic helpmeet: "We know many examples of great thinkers out there—men—who had a great woman behind them. This is actually quite typical in Thailand." Nilchawee's sister acknowledges, "It must not have been easy to be married to Sulak." Sulak also knows that his activist life created hardship and stress on Nilchawee and the family. He is grateful for her character and stalwart support: "My wife is very contented, and so kind. She is not overambitious. And she had never fussed about all my friends in the home or my workload. Even though she does not follow my radical way of thinking, she has always been there for me. I must have had good karma to have met her."

A few years after their marriage, Sulak opened the first alternative bookstore in Thailand, called Suksit Siam (Intellectual Siam), along the bustling King Rama IV Road. It was across the street from a crematorium operated by a Buddhist temple. Many people cautioned Sulak not to open a business in that inauspicious location, where ghosts might cross the street and enter the shop. With his modern sensibility, Sulak dismissed such superstitious talk.

What the *Social Science Review* had done for bringing an intellectual edge into print form, the opening of Suksit Siam in 1967 did as a meeting space for discussing ideas. The bookstore immediately became a hub for cultural, Buddhist, interreligious, and educational activities in Bangkok that promoted critical thinking and social reform,

arousing suspicion among the generals who kept an eye on such movements.

The second floor of the Suksit Siam building served as a meeting place where recent university graduates came to converse and debate. "Those who did not want to enter the mainstream came to the bookshop," Sulak recalls. "The students wanted to discuss what they were actually seeing and experiencing in society. Nothing was off limits. They wanted space for authentic discussion, and not just parroting what they were supposed to say."

A nucleus of students and graduates soon formed a small discussion group called a *sapha kafae*, or coffee house council, with Sulak as the informal adviser. Similar discussion groups emerged on university campuses around Bangkok, as the prohibition on public assembly had relaxed slightly under the Thanom regime. Sulak was invited to speak to nearly all of the student groups on wide-ranging topics. During this initial period of the bookstore and discussion groups, Sulak also became the editor of *Visakha Puja*, the annual publication in English of the Buddhist Association of Thailand; this position would continue for the next thirteen years.

As Sulak became well known in Thailand as a publisher, an increasing number of writers came to him to ask how they could get their works published. Sulak sought the advice of one of Thailand's most highly respected scholars, his mentor Phya Anuman. Sulak had read all of Phya Anuman's many works, which included ethnography, linguistics, and anthropology, and also studied his extensive writings about village

Previous page, top: Prince Sitthiporn blessed Sulak on his 36th birthday overlooked by Princess Chongchit.

Previous page, bottom: Phya Anuman (*with dark glasses*), Sulak and Prof. William Klausner at the Siam Society.

cultural life. There are very few people who Sulak believes are truly worthy of being called heroes, but for him, Phya Anuman (who died in 1969) was a true hero because he linked his countrymen and countrywomen to their Siamese roots. This was a heroic endeavor in Sulak's eyes. Sulak was a high school student when he first met Anuman, and they regularly corresponded while he was studying in the UK. After Sulak's return to Thailand, he was invited to share many Sunday morning discussions with Anuman. "Eventually I became like family at his home."

Herbert P. Phillips describes in *Modern Thai Literature* the occasion when Sulak approached Phya Anuman for training in literary criticism and social analysis: "The formality of their relationship was solemnized in a ritual in which Sulak literally prostrated himself before his teacher, swearing fealty and dutifulness. From that time on, Phya Anuman considered Sulak, both privately and publicly, his principal intellectual heir."

Sulak recognized the relationships that made him part of an intellectual genealogy, extending from those who inspired him and then, through himself, to those he inspired in turn. Phillips writes, "Sulak's link to Phya Anuman projected him further back into Thai history through Phya Anuman's own links to Prince Damrong (who had been Phya Anuman's supervisor and predecessor at the National Library). . . It was this series of direct, personal connections to a golden age of Thai scholar-bureaucrats that provided the emotional support and justification for the

Previous page, top: Sulak and Nilchawee standing behind Sulak's former teachers from Assumption College, including Brother François Hilaire (*right*).

Previous page, bottom: The Suksit Siam bookshop opened in 1967 with the old Siamese national flag with the white elephant.

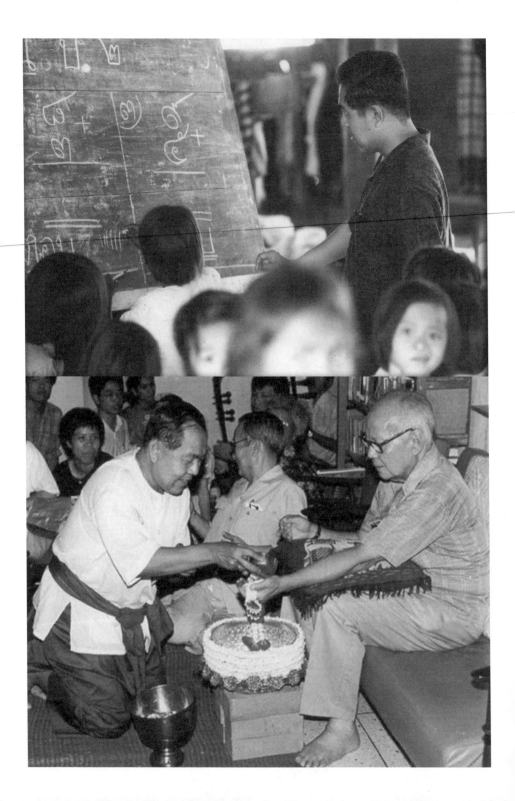

intellectual position that Sulak tried to establish for himself, with considerable success, during the 1960s and 1970s."

Phya Anuman agreed to help Sulak by donating the royalties from his own books to set up a foundation to support aspiring writers and artists. Additionally, Sulak obtained support from the family of Phra Saraprasert, another prominent scholar, who had recently passed away. The Sathirakoses-Nagapradipa Foundation was thus launched in 1968 in honor of the two great scholars: Sathirakoses was Phya Anuman's family name, and Nagapradipa was Phra Saraprasert's family name. The principal outlet for writers supported by the foundation was a magazine that Sulak revived, called *Pajarayasara* (Teacher of All Teachers). Sulak appointed his closest acolyte, Pibhop Dhongchai, as the first editor in 1968. Some forty-five years after its first issue and many different editors, in 2014 sixteen-year-old Netiwit "Frank" Chotiphatphaisal, Thailand's first publicly declared conscientious objector and an acolyte of Sulak's, took over the editorship of *Pajarayasara*.

The mid-1960s were a busy and productive time for Sulak. He was editing and writing at the *Review*, publishing *Pajarayasara*, running Suksit Siam with Nilchawee, continuing to teach at different universities, and frequently invited by Catholic and Protestant missionaries to give lectures to student groups about ethics, history, and Siamese culture. Of particular note, his work with Rev. Ray Downs at the Student Christian Center in Bangkok gave rise to a dynamic discussion group for both

Previous page, top: Sulak teaching Thai villagers in 1971.

Previous page, bottom: Sulak and Dr. Puey Ungphakorn performing a traditional benediction for the Siamese New Year.

Christian and Buddhist students, holding seminars such as "Youth's Social and Ethical Responsibility for Siam."

Because of the increasing number of participants in this popular group, a larger meeting space was needed, but one where the police would not intervene, since large public gatherings were still banned. Sulak was friendly with the abbot of Wat Boworniwet, who allowed them to use one of the temple buildings that was in disrepair. Sulak and the students repaired the building and cleaned the adjacent courtyard. When he told them the agendas for the meetings were in their hands, they responded by asking Sulak to conduct workshops, teach English, and facilitate political debates. Sulak arranged for esteemed academic and civil society leaders to give talks on cultural subjects, as well as to openly discuss the state of the country. Soon the club produced the *Social Science Review—Student Edition*, the first in the country, giving expression to young voices of dissent against the establishment. The Student Christian Center became one of the most vibrant gathering spaces in the city. Among the participants from Sulak's circle at the Center were several students who became leaders of the popular uprising of October 1973, as well as students who became involved in political movements that are active today, including the opposing "Red Shirts" and "Yellow Shirts."

Sulak's writings, dynamic leadership, and encouragement to students resonated beyond the young people and into society. His call to deeply study one's cultural roots, critically analyze the crisis in society, and above all, think independently, had far-reaching consequences in the following decades.

....

Phra Payutto offering a Buddhist discourse, with Sulak
seated below.

Angkarn Kalayanapong sketching Sulak.

Chapter 4

Two Monks and an Artist

In reviewing the events of Sulak's life in the later 1960s, one can see how significant his relationships were—ranging from his role as mentor and teacher of close followers, to his reciprocal bonds with "spiritual friends," to his contacts with progressive and unconventional figures of the cultural and religious worlds—in shaping Sulak's evolving vision.

By the late 1960s, Sulak had attained to the status of a respected teacher, addressed by the title Ajahn (or Arjan). Students flocked to him because of his dynamism and his openness to young people, and especially because he was willing to challenge mainstream culture. In Thailand it has been a time-honored tradition for a mentor, whether a monk or a layperson, to transmit teachings, skills, and wisdom to a group of followers. "The whole process of a real education depends on the teacher-disciple relationship," Sulak states. "And modern education has broken that relationship."

Students would often gather at his home, sitting on bamboo chairs and mats in the palm-leaf courtyard. There were around twenty who were very close and met with Sulak regularly. Other students, numbering in the hundreds, faded in and out according to their inclination and specific project involvement. Sulak nearly always led the activity in dreaming, envisioning, planning, and executing; but once a project began—such as publishing a magazine or book, planning a commemorative event, or founding a new organization—he empowered the students with its primary responsibilities. Sulak fostered an open forum in which the group could appraise and critique each other's work and writing, debate different political views, and develop a sense of camaraderie. These student groups were a frequent presence in the home, a tradition that continues to this day. Nilchawee would bring plates of fruit in the morning, and noodles in the afternoon. A roasted oolong was usually served throughout the day, while Sulak offered wine to those students who came in the evening to converse or work on the magazine. Rollout mattresses and mosquito netting were stored in the closet of his library room, in case any students needed a place to stay temporarily.

Sulak empowered his young followers to examine society and culture with a critical eye, to be skeptical of authority, and to have the courage to speak directly and without fear. He encouraged them to regularly assess themselves with naked honesty, to check whether their actions were in line with their aspirations and ideals—a practice that he himself followed. Followers were given freedom to challenge the teacher on his own behavior; this was unusual for Ajahns in Thailand and set Sulak apart from all other teachers. Engaging in open communication was part of Sulak's understanding of the Buddhist term *kalyana-mittata*, or spiritual friendship. The key to being an authentic spiritual friend (*kalyana-mitta*), according to Sulak, is to remain honest with oneself and others. "Good friends will tell you what you don't want to hear," students often heard him say.

Sulak seeks to practice his modern-day interpretation of kalyana-mittata not only with students but also with friends and work colleagues. In his book *Religion and Development* (1986), he writes, "A Good Friend would be one's 'other voice' of conscience, to put one on the proper path of development so that one would not escape from society, nor would one want to improve society in order to claim it as one's own achievement." Sulak admits to having a sizable ego, yet he remains open to the criticism of his kalyana-mitta if he is not walking his talk. Sulak hears regularly from these friends about his limitations—his temper, impatience, high-handedness, and fondness for red wine. Even those who are quick to point out Sulak's apparent failings admit that he can criticize himself just as quickly as he points out shortcomings in others.

Sulak's understanding of kalyana-mittata inspires loyalty among those with whom he works, even though his closest colleagues are not spared his sharp appraisals. However, on numerous occasions, Sulak's words or behaviors have been too powerful, causing some within his inner circle to part ways with him. A refrain of prominent Thai activists who know Sulak well is: "I support Sulak in his work, but will do so from afar. I don't want him as my boss." Rosana Tositrakul, Thailand's senator for Bangkok and one of Sulak's closest female acolytes, has acknowledged, "Ajahn Sulak is the angry type; that is just his personality. [But] he has never stopped engaging the younger generation, and this is a great quality."

Sulak was achieving increasing influence through the *Social Science Review* as well as his publications and lectures. The fame and prestige these activities brought were greatly satisfying to him. Though he tried to keep his feelings of superiority in check, humility was a challenge with so much adoration from young students, especially the close acolytes who eagerly assisted him with his work. Nonetheless, Sulak took seriously the traditional role of an Ajahn, supporting the acolytes and guiding their lives as a mentor, by helping them find professional opportunities or employment, arranging monastic ordination, publishing their writings and finding venues for their art, and above all, encouraging their curiosity and intellect. Of the hundreds of students who have sought him out over the years, Sulak says, "From a Buddhist perspective, there must be a karmic connection from past lives. But clearly, they come because we share a concern for the poor and we want to stand with the oppressed.

"Whoever comes to me, if they come for food I give them rice at my table. If they want tea, I pour them tea. If they want articles to read, I give them books. I give them whatever they want. I don't look for anything from them. Some ask for more and some ask for less. Money is nothing. If I have money, I give it to them, no problem. The most precious, though, is when they ask for my time. Over the years, it is with my time that I've been most generous."

During Sulak's six years as editor of the *Review* (1963–1969), he traveled throughout Thailand to interview scholars and abbots, and to ask princes and monks and poets to contribute original works. He often invited his acolytes to accompany him so that they could be exposed the nation's varied people and places beyond Bangkok, and to open their minds and hearts to the common people.

Sulak Sivaraksa and the Path of Socially Engaged Buddhism

During this period of his editorship, Sulak connected with three men who were significant both to him personally and for the benefit of his students. Two of them were Buddhist monks—Bhikkhu Buddhadasa and Prayudh Payutto—and the third was the poet-painter Angkarn Kalayanapong. All three profoundly affected Sulak's socially engaged Buddhism as it began to emerge in the 1980s.

If the 1960s had been a decade of intellectual flourishing for Sulak, the 1970s would see him applying his intellect to help others. And Buddhadasa, Payutto, and Angkarn, in different ways, spurred this action.

Buddhadasa was the most radical monk Thailand had ever produced. Sulak was not initially drawn to his reformist Buddhism. When it came to Theravada Buddhism, Sulak was not one to rock the boat in the early 1960s. Like most Thai, Sulak adhered to a conservative presentation of Theravada Buddhism, one that did not emphasize transcendence, individual meditative experience, or philosophical inquiry. Instead, the focus for the great majority of Thai Buddhists was prayer, devotional practice, and daily meritorious actions, such as offering food to monks.

Buddhadasa was extremely humble but also very confident. In the late 1950s, when he gave a series of lectures on Buddhist practice in Bangkok, he shocked the nation with his unconventional behavior: standing at a lectern instead of sitting completely still on a decorated dais, and gesturing in a spirited way instead of speaking with no emotion. Buddhadasa suggested at his lectures that statues of the Buddha were obstructing the actual practice of the Dhamma—another shock, in a county where prayers and offerings are made daily before beloved golden images in thousands of Buddhist temples and shrines. He said that the worship of statues promoted materialism and idolatry, even pointing at a statue with his cane, usually an offensive gesture. To the gasp of the audience, he declared, "We can drown all the Buddha images in the Chao

Phraya," the large river flowing through Bangkok. This was Buddhadasa's way of challenging people to renounce their blind faith in dogma and ritual, in favor of practices that empower individuals with meditative experience.

Sulak was displeased when reports of these notorious lectures came to his attention while he was in England: "Buddhadasa said that the Buddha statues are like mountains obscuring real Buddhist practice! I felt he was going too far." Buddhadasa's teachings were too radical for Sulak. As with his views toward the monarchy, it took time for Sulak's fixed ideas about Buddhism to be reshaped.

Buddhadasa's Suan Mokkh hermitage in the Chaiya district of southern Thailand, established in 1932, became a destination for thousands of devotees, lay and monastic, including a number of Western students. Buddhadasa wanted Suan Mokkh to be an environment in which the original teachings of the Buddha would be revived, and he saw it as more a place for community development than for individual retreat from the world. He wanted the Dhamma to be relevant and applicable to modern culture. Buddhadasa lived a simple life in tune with nature, meditating in the jungle in the mornings and writing about modernity and the Dhamma in the afternoon. Even though his teachings were challenging, Buddhadasa had a hands-off style as a teacher and administrator, allowing his students to find their own path and create their own practice and study. He was open to learning from the Mahayana and Vajrayana Buddhist traditions, and even other religions—a strikingly progressive attitude in Thailand, which on the whole had a sectarian bias toward Theravada Buddhism.

Opposite page: Sulak with Bhikkhu Buddhadasa at his monastery at Suan Mokkh.

His devotees published Buddhadasa's many talks and writings, including *Tam Roi Phra Arahant* (Following the Path of the Arhats), which Sulak picked up by chance in 1964. On reading it, something finally clicked in Sulak's mind. "That book got me! His writing was so clear, especially when he suggested that even in today's modern world, all of us—woman and man, monastic and layperson—can follow in the footsteps of the *arhats*, the great practitioners of the Buddhist path. No teachers were saying that at the time. I wanted to meet him. He was so sharp and progressive, and he was ready to use new ways to express the Dhamma."

"It is Buddhadasa's creativity and generous interpretations that have often made him the focus of criticism," says Prof. Grant Olson, writing in the preface to his translation of *Buddhadhamma* by Prayudh Payutto. "His [Buddhadasa's] liberal comparison of Buddhism and Christianity, equating Dhamma with God, raised the eyebrows of many conservative Theravada Buddhists."

Sulak decided to feature Buddhadasa in the *Review*. Accompanied by one of his students, Sulak traveled to Suan Mokkh, first by train and then walking for an hour in the jungle, to meet the monk, then sixty years old. There was an immediate bond. Like any Thai, Sulak paid respects by bowing at Buddhadasa's feet, yet their bond was not that of master and disciple, but between inquiring minds. Easily shifting to his intellectual mode, he began questioning Buddhadasa on a variety of topical issues: the declining state of the monkhood in Thailand; new ways to offer Buddhist teachings through cinema, music, and illustrated books; and how all religions converge on one essential point: minimizing self-importance. Interviewing Buddhadasa like a BBC reporter, Sulak preserved the conversation on a tape recording, the transcript of which would accompany Sulak's article on Buddhadasa in the next *Review* issue. After this first meeting, they continued to communicate frequently by letter, and when Buddhadasa came to Bangkok, Sulak took him around the city. Sulak also accompanied Buddhadasa on a two-week teaching tour by boat throughout the islands of southern Thailand.

Sulak came to appreciate Buddhadasa's great scholarship, deep meditation practice, and unique presentation of the Dhamma. Buddhadasa rejected much of the official state-sponsored curriculum of study for monks, and demythologized the teachings of the Buddha. His was a practical and innovative approach for both monks and laity that involved combining a personal meditation practice with an active engagement with society. Both Mahayana Buddhism and Christianity, especially his reading of Christian humility, influenced Buddhadasa. His teachings emphasized the Mahayana path of the *bodhisattva*, in which the aspirant aspires to bring freedom from suffering to all beings, not just oneself. By contrast, Theravada Buddhism, the oldest form of Buddhism, based on the Pali-language canon, emphasizes the spiritual liberation of the individual as an *arhat* more than the bodhisattva ideal. Under the influence of Buddhadasa, Sulak in time adopted a more Mahayana attitude toward his spiritual path, and eventually he studied with Mahayana teachers including Thich Nhat Hanh and Tibetan lamas.

Buddhadasa did not separate the individual's spiritual path from the needs of society. He was the first monk in Thailand to teach about the intersection of Buddhism and politics. Such a view hardly won the favor of the Buddhist ecclesiastical hierarchy, but he was careful not to criticize officials or politicians by name; as he told Sulak, "I don't want to be crucified like Jesus Christ!" It was risky for Buddhadasa or any other monk to speak frankly because of the very real threat of arrest or disappearance under the Thai authority or at the hands of Communist guerrillas.

Two prominent and competing worldviews in Thailand in the late 1960s and '70s were the frequent butt of Buddhadasa's criticism: what he called "vengeful Marxism" and "bloodthirsty capitalists." As a response to the crisis in Thai society brought on by dictators, repeated coups, the growing military, and political corruption, Buddhadasa taught "Dhammic Socialism," a path to societal renewal. This was not the materialistic socialism promoted by Marxists, but rather a moral system built on a foundation of spiritual practice. Its principles stress the diminishment of the self-cherishing ego and the understanding that every being's welfare is interrelated with that of every other being. Sulak describes Dhammic Socialism as being "not the socialism of the Soviet Union or China, but a real socialism of democracy, fraternity, equality, and liberty, like the community the Buddha had founded." The scholar of religion Donald Swearer wrote in the introduction to Buddhadasa's *Dhammic Socialism* (1986) that the monk had long been "a severe critic of Thai Buddhism, especially its preoccupation with empty ceremonial and magical ritual. He has urged a return to an authentic *Buddha-dhamma*, replacing merit-making with a serious quest for Nirvana, the memorization of endless categories of Abhidhamma philosophies with an understanding of the Suttas, the performance of magical rituals with the practice of meditation, and an undue emphasis on the monk with a concern for the entire Buddhist community, lay and monastic."

Buddhadasa wrote in one of his essays collected in *Me and Mine* (1991) that "the socialist ideal of Buddhism finds expression in the concept of the bodhisattva. The bodhisattva is one who not only helps others, but sacrifices himself, even his own life, for others. Buddhism upholds this ideal because of the socialist intention which prevails throughout all aspects of the tradition."

As Buddhadasa's influence grew, Kukrit Pramoj, who was the very epitome of the Thai elite and aristocrats, sought to debate him publicly. As described by Baker and Phongpaichit in *A History of Thailand*,

"Kukrit represented a marriage of free-market capitalism, elitist democracy, exemplary monarchy, and paternalist government which appealed to many businessmen and urban middle class as a route beyond military rule." Kukrit and other elites were deeply attached to a strict social order and worked to maintain it. They did not want Buddhadasa's popular message of bringing the Buddha's teachings into society to spread, because it would threaten the social order. Kukrit and Buddhadasa, two intellectual giants, held a series of debates between 1963 and 1965 that attracted large radio audiences.

The debates started out on a cordial note, but soon Kukrit was frustrated with his inability to dislodge Buddhadasa from his dialectic. In essence their disagreement rested on the question of whether one can live in the world, contributing positively to society, while also practicing the Dhamma, including the attainment of deep states of meditative absorption. Kukrit insisted it was impossible. Citing a popular slogan promoted by Prime Minister Sarit—"Work is money; money is work"— Kukrit suggested that contentment was not a worthy virtue in individuals since it did not encourage the development of society. Kukrit believed that anyone who wants to walk the path of the Buddha must necessarily reject the world. Buddhadasa believed the contrary, that in order to make true and long-lasting contributions to society, the most efficient way is to be free of one's self-cherishing ego. Relinquishing the ego would bring about a deep understanding of the Buddhist principle of interdependence and thus give rise to immeasurable compassion that would motivate positive changes in society.

Eventually, in the 1970s, Kukrit began to lash out at Buddhadasa's teachings. Tomomi Ito writes in *Modern Thai Buddhism and Buddhadasa Bhikkhu* (2012), "Beyond his emotional antagonism toward Buddhadasa, Kukrit wrote a number of essays, especially in his newspaper, *Sayam Rat*

[Siam Rath], opposing Buddhadasa, and suggested the monk's teachings were "an evil to the development of the nation" and "could endanger national security." Both men continued to write about their respective positions—Kukrit in his newspaper and Buddhadasa in books—and criticized each other, especially Kukrit's advancement of capitalism and Buddhadasa's promotion of Dhammic Socialism.

Sulak did not agree with everything Buddhadasa proposed in *Dhammic Socialism*; nonetheless, more than any thinker or politician, it was Buddhadasa whose teachings Sulak integrated and promoted in his articulation of a socially engaged Buddhism in the 1980s.

Sulak related the story of how, in 1993, when Buddhadasa was close to death, his attendant requested some final words of advice. The words were: "Rest in the luminous aspect of the mind. And read *Present Moment Wonderful Moment*." Sulak explained, "I had translated and published from English into Thai that book by Thich Nhat Hanh, *Present Moment Wonderful Moment*. I felt very happy, and have since given that book to so many people before they engage in political demonstrations.

"Still, when Buddhadasa died, I felt as if a mountain had collapsed, or the biggest tree in the forest had fallen," Sulak said. "But at the same time, because I'm Buddhist, I used the opportunity to contemplate impermanence."

The second monk with whom Sulak collaborated and who significantly influenced him was Prayudh Payutto, who is now celebrated as Thailand's foremost Buddhist scholar and who in 2016 was promoted to the *Mahathera Samakhom*, or Supreme Sangha Council, the highest governing body for monks in Thailand. But when Sulak met him in 1969, the monk was an administrator at Chulalongkorn University and not widely known. Sulak asked Payutto to contribute an article to an issue of the *Review*, in

Sulak Sivaraksa and the Path of Socially Engaged Buddhism

collaboration with the Siam Society and the Buddhist Society of Thailand, devoted to the role of Buddhism in contemporary society. Payutto's contribution, titled "The Problem of Status and Activities of the Monkhood," brought high praise from academics and scholars of Buddhism. Sulak views their collaboration at the *Review* as the launching pad for Payutto's major work, and claims credit for discovering his genius. Sulak agreed with Payutto that the role of monks in society needed to be completely reformed in a manner that would bring monks *into* society, with activities such as social work, rather than remaining inert in city temples or isolated in forest hermitages. Payutto argued that the institution of ordained monkhood could only be preserved by adapting it to the needs of modern society.

In 1971, Sulak commissioned Payutto to write a short article on Buddhist philosophy for a Festschrift honoring Prince Wan Waithayakon. Payutto later expanded on the article to produce his magnum opus, *Phutthatham (Buddhadhamma)*, distilling the essential teachings of the Pali canon. *Buddhadhamma* is widely appreciated as the finest textually grounded, contemporary interpretation of Theravada Buddhism. Prof. Grant Olson, whose English translation of the book was published in 1995, called the work "a masterpiece of modern Buddhist scholarship and Thai literature" and "the most significant Thai contribution to Buddhist scholarship in the last 200 years."

Even the scrupulous Sulak could find little to criticize in the book and adopted it as a guide to what he felt were the most important Buddhist aspects of the Siamese identity. Payutto often acknowledged Sulak as being the original spark for the creation of *Buddhadhamma*. They have maintained a close friendship throughout their lives.

Payutto went on to publish widely, from detailed commentaries on the Buddhist scriptures and monastic discipline to Buddhist critiques of modern challenges, including environmental degradation, the appropriate use of technology, and inequitable national economic policy. Taking Buddhadasa as an inspiration, he was a doctrinal and institutional reformer. But whereas Buddhadasa looked to other Buddhist traditions and religions for alternative models, Payutto chose to draw only on the Pali canon. If there is one criticism from Sulak, it is that Payutto was somewhat sectarian, or at least did not refer to other Buddhist schools, notably the Mahayana. Payutto worked within the Theravada system, while Buddhadasa worked outside it. Payutto was not inclined to challenge political authority directly and did not provoke the ire of the military dictators or politicians as Buddhadasa did.

Sulak carefully studied Payutto's corpus of writings, and they held long discussions on the applicability of the Dhamma to society and how to promote ethics and values in development and modernity. Their subjects included the responsibility of the individual to society, the commitment of the meditator to the nation-state, and the application of personal insights for the greater good. As Payutto wrote in *Buddhadhamma*, "Buddhism regards both the person and the system, both the individual and society, both the external environment and the internal mind, as important. [Both sides] have to work with and complement each other." All these themes Sulak wove into his later articulation of a socially engaged Buddhism.

The third significant person encountered by Sulak through his *Review* work was the reclusive and controversial poet and painter Angkarn Kalayanapong. They first met in 1958 when Sulak returned temporarily from England. Together they went on pilgrimage to the ruins of the temples, monasteries, and sculptures of the ancient capital of Ayutthaya. Sulak was attracted by Angkarn's love and expert knowledge of Ayutthaya arts and culture, and his unrestrained eccentricity. He studied at Silpakorn University's art department under Prof. Silp Bhirasri, a native Italian who pioneered the modern art movement in Thailand. But Angkarn was eventually thrown out because university officials couldn't bear his unconventional behavior. Angkarn became an accomplished surrealist who used charcoal and watercolor in mural-like dreamscapes of Buddhist and temple imagery. At the time he and Sulak met, Angkarn was also publishing poetry, and Sulak knew of his reputation for unorthodox language and contravention of poetic norms. But even though his verse was lambasted by mainstream critics, Sulak invited Angkarn to contribute poems to the *Review*, as well as charcoal drawings created for the cover of the some of the first issues.

Most Thai poets in the 1960s and '70s wrote pedestrian works for the monarchy or elite. There were also a few prominent leftist poets displaying a distinctly Thai Marxist ideology in their work. Angkarn was unlike any of these poets. He held disdain for King Bhumibol, whom he often called blind because the King did not read poetry, and he found politics tedious. Angkarn's poetry, especially his *nirat*, a travelogue genre, paid homage to Siamese roots and mourned the present day by contrasting it with the glorious Ayutthaya period some four hundred years in the past. He was an idealist and lived to inspire through aesthetics. Just as he had helped promote the work of Payutto, Sulak brought Angkarn to public attention and gave him a national platform for his art, poetry, and essays, first through the *Review* and later through other publications and venues. Sulak was first and foremost a friend to Angkarn, but also his chief promoter and a collector of his art. Eventually Angkarn gained national prominence, in 1989 receiving the title of National Artist of Thailand for that year. Some of his most famous works hang in Sulak's home in Bangkok.

"He regarded me as his patron," said Sulak. "I was helping him all through his life, and the foundations I set up supported him. I bought him land. Got him out of debt. Bought his art. But money had no meaning for Angkarn. When he got a lot of money, he would buy food and feed all the street dogs. He was crazy with no pretentions. A completely genuine person. You can see that in his poetry. He spoke to plants and frogs. He would look at stones, and he could hear the stones speaking to him."

Angkarn stayed often at Sulak's home and was exposed to his wide circle of acolytes and friends, intellectuals, activists, writers, artists, monks, and international connections. Angkarn was sometimes anti-social, but Sulak placed him in the middle of his world. Once, when the American Beat poet Allen Ginsberg was visiting Bangkok, the cultural attaché from the US embassy stopped by Sulak's home to ask if there were any "Thai Beat poets" to introduce to Ginsberg. "I knew Ginsberg and Angkarn would get along. I introduced them and they were mad together. Drinking and reciting poetry," Sulak recalls. "Ginsberg and Angkarn were so similar."

Angkarn and Sulak remained friends for decades. When Angkarn was gravely ill from heart disease in August 2012, Sulak was called to his hospital bedside. The poet had been comatose for some days, and the doctors thought he would pass in a matter of hours. Yet Angkarn returned to consciousness when Sulak began to speak to him, reminding him, "The work of real poets is timeless. You have that immortal quality."

"You won't ever die, Kuhn Angkarn," said Sulak (addressing Angkarn with a common courteous title), "because your poetry is immortal."

Angkarn smiled and opened his eyes. "Ah, you see, now I can finally die because Sulak says I'm immortal." A moment of light entered the poet's eyes as he looked toward his daughters standing nearby.

Within minutes of Sulak's walking out of the hospital room, Angkarn took his last breath.

Historians have noted that the revitalized spirit of intellectual curiosity, skepticism, and creative license that began in Thailand in the 1960s may be attributed directly to the energetic work, writings, and contributions of Sulak and his circle at the *Review*. In 1969, after six years as its editor, Sulak stepped away, though he remained on the editorial board. He handed over the editor position to Suchat Sawatsri. The *Review* was eventually banned by authorities following the massacre of students on 6 October 1976.

More than fifty years after Sulak founded the *Review*, he believes that his most significant lifetime contributions to Thai society included bringing Payutto and Angkarn out of their reclusive corners.

"Angkarn and Payutto probably would have become popular anyhow, but the fact is that I pushed them initially and was the sower of these seeds, the originator of these two great individuals. So I have some sense of accomplishment in that."

Just as Sulak was energized by the luminaries he met, so in turn was Sulak's circle of acolytes inspired by him. The ability to identify untapped potential in the younger generation is one of Sulak's most perceptive traits. As Anchalee Kurutach of the Buddhist Peace Fellowship says, "It is Sulak's special quality of his heart and mind to recognize [people with] potential and connect them with fellow students and activists, and with action where they can make a difference in society." One such person was an idealistic and enthusiastic young man named Komol Keemthong, a recent graduate from the prestigious Chulalongkorn University, whom he met in 1971. Sulak didn't have to look too deeply to see that this was a special individual. Komol spent time with Sulak and worked on student editions of the *Review*. Eventually he asked Sulak for advice about whether he should accept the offer of an academic lectureship at his alma mater.

"So much of what we do is superficial," Sulak told Komol. "You need to get deep down to know the country, to know our culture, and to open yourself to the poor."

Heeding Sulak's advice, Komol decided to start a school for poor children in the south of Thailand. The Thai Communist Party was strong in the area and had many camps in the jungle near where Komol was teaching. Komol knew that if his presence was unwelcome to the Communists, they would warn him to leave. Sulak was worried about Komol before he left. Komol subsequently wrote to Sulak to report that the school had been an immediate success. He wrote about how he was bringing in local artists and musicians to teach, and confided that his girlfriend had joined him to work at the school.

On a trip to Bangkok, Komol visited with Sulak and asked to borrow a tape recorder and camera. Sulak warned him that he should not be seen with these devices in the jungle because the Communist rebels, who were actively fighting the Thai military, would suspect him of being a government agent from Bangkok.

Komol reassured Sulak, "I'll be OK. The Communists down there always warn us to leave at least three times. They know I'm just a teacher."

One week later, Sulak received a telephone call informing him that Komol and his girlfriend had been shot dead by Communist guerrillas.

"I collapsed when I heard the news," Sulak said. "Without me, he might not have died in that way. He wanted to dig deep in life, and he died for that."

Shortly after the tragic murders, the work of establishing a foundation to honor Komol was begun. Sulak joined with Prof. Sanya Dharmasakti, a judge and politician who was then president of the Buddhist Association of Thailand, and Dr. Puey Ungphakorn, a prominent economist, to establish the Komol Keemthong Foundation. The Komol Keemthong Foundation, Sulak believes, was the first large-scale social action organization in Thailand. "Our main objective was to promote idealism among the young so that they would dedicate themselves to work for the people," Sulak says. "And we tried to revive Buddhist values."

Komol represented for Sulak the best of the young intellectuals who were seeking to understand their heritage and to uplift their people through education. In connection with Komol's cremation ceremony, Sulak published a small commemorative volume, in which he shared the last letter that Komol had sent to him from the jungles of southern Thailand. In it, the young idealist wrote:

"For a bridge to be built over a tumultuous river, we must set the first foundational brick. And I might be that first one."

....

Over 400,000 Thais demonstrated in the streets of Bangkok on
14 October 1973.

Chapter 5

Siam's Bloodiest Days

October of 1973 found Sulak in Singapore meeting with other progressive-minded leaders and activists for a project called Cultural Relations for the Future. The two-year project was sponsored by the small US-based Hazen Foundation "to study and find solutions to the world's most pressing problems," as Sulak recalls. He was the chair of the Southeast Asia group, and in the final report to the foundation, the group concluded that cultural relations are "the chief means to shape the future of men and nations, to change their directions through create mutual borrowing and to strengthen an awareness of shared values. . . . Mankind is faced with problems which, if not dealt with, could in a very few years develop into crises world-wide in scope. Interdependence is the reality; world-wide problems the prospect; and world-wide cooperation the only solution."

While Sulak was in Singapore, he heard there was unrest in Bangkok and that government forces had fired upon students. Sulak rushed home on the next flight.

When he disembarked in Bangkok, the airport was eerily quiet, with only a few planes on the tarmac and very few people in the terminal. There were no government workers at their posts. Sulak walked by the unattended desks of custom agents, aware that something drastic had happened. When he arrived at home, his wife and some of his students whisked him to an in-law's house, fearful that the Thai authorities might come to arrest him. Sulak was told that a popular uprising was unfolding, with hundreds of thousands of people in the street. They turned on the radio to listen for any official news.

Sulak was not surprised the revolt was being led by students calling for democratic reforms and a constitution. The protests were on a scale never before seen in Thailand and were partly a response to the decades of authoritarian rule under the Phibun, Sarit, and Thanom military regimes. It was also a result of the intellectual awakening of students over the previous decade, in which the *Social Science Review* played a significant role. Leftist political ideology, which opposed Thailand's support of America's war in Vietnam, and the tenfold increase in the number of students between 1961 and 1972 also contributed to the massive uprising of young people.

What happened in the days before Sulak returned to Bangkok? In the first days of October 1973, students and workers held a public demonstration to demand a new constitution. The Thanom government arrested a number of student leaders and accused them of plotting to overthrow the government. Sulak knew all of those arrested, including the secretary of the Komol Keemthong Foundation.

Over the next week, street protests swelled. Some 400,000 people from all walks of life marched to the Democracy Monument in the center of Bangkok and moved throughout the city, protesting the government's detainment of students. On 14 October, King Bhumibol interceded and issued a request that the students disband. Out of deference to the King, the students agreed. But in the confusion of attempting to communicate with masses of protesters, clashes broke out and the overly zealous police force opened fire. Seventy-seven people were killed and more than eight hundred were injured.

"This is the darkest day, the most sorry day in our history, because our own people were killed," King Bhumibol said on television.

While the King was sad, the people were angry. The next day, over half a million protesters filled the streets of Bangkok, calling for the resignation of the dictator Thanom. That evening, the King replaced Thanom with Sanya Dharmasakti as the new prime minister. By the next day, Thanom and his two advisers, Colonel Narong Kittikachorn (his son) and General Praphas Charusathien (his son's father-in-law)—collectively known as "the three tyrants"—had fled the country. The King allowed them to leave the country with the help of the military. Students were enraged, as they wanted Thanom and his cronies put on trial and imprisoned.

The 14 October popular uprising was a defining moment in the history of Thailand, for two reasons. First, it altered the Thai political system, reinstating democracy after decades of military rule. Second, it was the first time that the King of Thailand, who was believed to be above the political fray, became personally and directly involved with political matters. This fact was seized upon by royalists, who insisted that it was the King who threw out the dictator and restored civilian rule, not the students. Many Thai believed this false narrative.

However pleased Sulak was to see the dictator fall from power, he did not go so far as to give any credit to the King. Sulak's ideal of kingship was a virtuous and skillful monarch, but in King Bhumibol he saw only a weak man overwhelmed by his responsibilities. Sulak's view of the King was forever changed by 14 October; nonetheless, he held his tongue and refrained from publicly criticizing the King.

In the immediate aftermath of 14 October, Sulak's prestige was at its peak. His past *Review* editorials condemning the military rule were credited with informing the students and inspiring them to bring down Thanom and the generals. Sulak's writings were now seen almost as prophetic. Other writers who were critical of the military and whose writings were published by Sulak in the *Review* felt vindicated. The many seminars and discussion groups achieved results—they were not just talk; they broke the authoritarian grip on the nation. And Sulak had been at the center of it all, like a director of a traditional *khon* masked dance drama. Historians have noted the primary role that Sulak played at this watershed moment in Thailand, which Sulak also recognized. He wrote in *Siam in Crisis*, "During the student uprising against the military government, that these were my students, in a way it was true. They read the magazine (*Social Science Review*). They took part in clubs and seminars that grew out of the magazine. These were the students who were the leaders in 1973."

In the days after the protests, leaders of the uprising came to Sulak, expressing their delight that the generals were gone. "The students thought they had won," Sulak says. "I told them that the three tyrants had fled but the structure was still the same. The military still has control behind the scenes. Be careful, I warned, because they will come back to get you."

A feeling of jubilation and a sense of opportunity filled the air, but Sulak remained somber. "When I told the students they were wrong, that they had not won, I went from being their hero to their criticizing me for being old-fashioned and conservative."

A year later, in 1974, a new constitution was ratified, and political

Sulak Sivaraksa and the Path of Socially Engaged Buddhism

space opened for increased civil liberties, freedom of the press, and the work of nongovernmental organizations among the poor and factory workers. There was hopefulness among the democratic and humanitarian campaigners, especially the students and workers, though Sulak reminded them not to be complacent with their newfound democracy.

"It dawned upon me that unless the masses are empowered to influence politics and issues that affect their lives, the ruling elites, no matter how able or benevolent, can never bring the country an inch closer to democracy," Sulak wrote in *Powers That Be*. "Indeed, the rulers' philanthropy and benevolence sometimes mask brutal exploitation. Furthermore, a benevolent act is sometimes intended to perpetuate politics of dependency and the unjust status quo. A meaningful democracy requires structural and legal changes. In a way, democracy cannot be taught or imposed from above. It is a way of life, and hence only when we live democratically will we know what democracy is."

King Bhumibol hand-picked more than 2,500 individuals from across the professional and political spectrum, who were invited to a constitutional assembly at the Royal Turf Club. Sulak had been toying with the idea of entering politics at this time. When he surveyed potential candidates for prime minister, Sulak frankly could find no one more qualified than himself. But when his name did not appear on the list of those chosen for the assembly, Sulak quickly became bitter. Why was he not one of over 2,500 citizens invited for the constitution assembly? It is likely that his intellectual nemesis, Kukrit Pramoj, kept him out by directly influencing the King. Sulak contends that he would have chosen to remain outside the system, as a critic, and not be corrupted by political power games. Nonetheless, it must have been a blow to his ego that he was excluded from one of the most important political events in his adult life, when nearly every other leading intellectual, thinker, and politician in

Thailand was in attendance. By the end of the assembly, Kukrit had positioned himself perfectly and was elected its chairman, and in 1975 he became prime minister of Thailand. Though Kukrit implemented some progressive reforms, such as opening public housing and providing assistance to farmers, Sulak felt he did little of substance and railed against him as a duplicitous politician.

Within twelve months there was a new constitution, but disappointment soon followed. Infighting among the new political parties, corruption among the existing bureaucrats, and nepotism prevented the government programs or comprehensive reforms hoped for by the students and workers. Thailand experienced the messy work of a multiparty democracy. Sulak was discouraged by the government's failures and increasingly disheartened by the King, who he had hoped would emerge as a strong leader but sadly had not.

As the political wrangling continued in parliament, the Communist Party of Thailand was on the rise. Though they had already been in existence for twenty years, the CPT initiated their "People's War" in earnest with a guerrilla insurgency in 1965. The CPT was the second largest Communist movement in Southeast Asia, with more than 12,000 armed fighters at its height by the early 1970s. The party took its inspiration more from China than Russia, and established its base of operation among the Thai-Lao, among the non-Thai minorities in the mountains of the north and northeast, and among the Malay in the southern provinces. Old intellectuals, young artists, and students were their target recruits. China and North Vietnam provided Thai cadres with training, financial assistance, and arms for insurgency, subversion, and terrorism.

The Thai government's counteroffensive against the CPT, assisted by the United States, met with limited success. The Communists had gained moderate support in the impoverished rural communities, and also were energized by thousands of idealistic students who joined the CPT in the 1970s. Sulak knew many of these students who went to live in Communist camps and who took up arms. When some came to tell him they were leaving for the jungle, he replied that they were free to believe in any ideology, but he also warned them, "Many of you really believe in this horrible Marxist ideology that advocates armed struggle. But if you look at your Siamese roots, you will see that they are based on *ahimsa*, nonviolence. I know you will all return deeply disappointed, if you don't end up killed."

Concurrent with the government's limited reforms, and with their fight against the CPT, there was an increase in ultranationalist right-wing militants who identified Communists as their enemy. As in other countries during the Cold War, the right wing's paranoia about Communism extended beyond the guerrillas to include students, trade unions, and other progressives. Militants formed armed vigilante groups such as the Village Scouts and the Red Gaurs (*gaur* means a type of bull), which had the tacit approval of the Thai military and government. With the jingoistic vow to defend the revered values of Nation, Religion, and Monarchy, they targeted anyone suspected of the slightest sympathy toward Communism. Being labeled a Communist was serious; thousands of suspected people each year were harassed, assaulted, disappeared, lynched, and murdered.

Against the backdrop of the CPT in Thailand and the reactionary right-wing militants opposing Communism, the political sea change in October 1973 inspired thousands of students to work for social welfare programs. These students spawned Thailand's nongovernmental organization (NGO) movement. These NGOs served the poor and worked with farmers' movements, labor unions, and the underrepresented—the same demographic from which the Communists were trying to recruit. The

NGO movement was bolstered by financial support from the United States and Germany, and many Catholic and Protestant missionary and charity programs. There was broad idealism among youth who intended to better their communities and country—and now they saw concrete ways to do this through the NGOs. Right-wing militants immediately suspected the NGO workers of being Communist sympathizers. Sulak knew of this danger, as he himself was accused many times of being a Communist. Still, he and his students continued to work with and establish grassroots organizations. Decades later, historians would credit Sulak with starting the Thai indigenous NGO movement through his social welfare and development organizations.

Amid the rise in progressive and leftist publications—nearly all of which were accused of being Communist mouthpieces—Sulak formed a publishing and book distribution network, Klett Thai. Such a network was needed, he felt, because the few book distributors that existed in the early 1970s had no interest in books about progressive or cutting-edge ideas. When Sulak procured the financial backing for Klett Thai from a German textbook publishing house, Klett Verlag, he was in business. Sulak was tireless in creating and financing new outlets to bring his own, his students', and his colleagues' publications and ideas to the public. He wanted to create a resurgence in Siamese cultural identity, one that depended on neither American values nor Marxist ideology. Some have criticized Sulak for being associated directly with the US government, the World Bank, or corporations, all of whom he has regularly lambasted. Sulak sees no contradiction in taking money from capitalists or Western governments to support his and others' projects. Arun Senkuttuvan, an Indian journalist who has followed Sulak's lifelong work, said, "Sulak has never been averse to working with businesspeople, provided that they heard and shared his concerns, and supported him."

It was during this period after 1973 that Sulak began his transformation from intellectual and writer to active campaigner for social justice. Like his own students, he was shaped by what he learned from rural people and farmers. Sulak began to write and speak about the development of the country more than ever, and the role that Buddhism should play in directing the right course of action. Sulak stressed that development should be measured in spiritual progress and not only in material wealth.

When Sulak set out to advise the Graduate Volunteer Service program, which trained university students to work in rural development, he collaborated closely with the distinguished economist Dr. Puey Ungphakorn. An impeccably honest man, Dr. Puey represented the ideals of students, workers, and intellectuals alike. He had been appointed by the previous governments as Governor of the Bank of Thailand from 1957 to 1971. Sulak respected Dr. Puey's work on behalf of his fellow Thai in promoting property law reforms, an income redistribution policy, and fair pricing in the agriculture industry. Dr. Puey, in his very measured manner, constantly called out corruption in the bureaucracy of government, and had been forced to flee into exile in 1972 by the dictator Thanom. He returned after 14 October 1973 to become the rector of Thammasat University, and was appointed the Chairman of the Economic Advisers to the Prime Minister in 1974.

Puey arranged for a meeting with King Bhumibol for Sulak and others who were involved in writing and publishing. They were trying to maintain cordial relations with the palace, in order to navigate the difficult terrain that intellectuals and agents of social change had to tread in Thailand. Sulak's view of the King was becoming increasingly critical.

"I saw how the King had an inferiority complex in relation to intellectuals because he never really studied [at university] or got a degree. During our royal audience, he did the usual thing where he preaches about matters he knows little about, and spoke about the ease and luxury of the life of writers, publishers, and booksellers."

In response, Sulak reports that he said, "Your Majesty, it may be easy, but only for you because you are the King. For us normal writers it is very difficult."

Dr. Puey knew Sulak was candid but had not suspected he would speak in such a frank manner with the King. He was also surprised that Sulak was able to do so in the unique royal dialect.

"The King got angry with my comment, and our audience ended." It was Sulak's last face-to-face meeting with King Bhumibol.

In 1975 Sulak invited Dr. Puey to participate in a seminar and fact-finding mission in Isan, the northeastern region of Thailand, on the border with Laos. The seminar concerned the proposed Pha Mong Dam across the Mekong River. The dam project was controversial because of the thousands of villagers it would displace, a situation that other dams along the Mekong had already caused elsewhere. Sulak and Stewart Meacham, a peace activist working for the American Friends Service Committee (AFSC), were the organizers of the seminar, which was sponsored by the Komol Keemthong Foundation.

Sulak's work with the AFSC and the Quakers in Thailand, as well as in the Philippines, India, Sri Lanka, and Japan, propelled him more into the role of an activist. "I found the Quakers to be even more articulate than Buddhists on why we need to question and resist the powers of the state," he says. "If the state supports violence, we must resist. Buddhists in my country and elsewhere have for too long coexisted with nation-states that perpetuate violence." It was the Quakers' convincing articulation of nonviolence that led Sulak to question his long-held conservative beliefs and support of sacrosanct institutions, namely the monarchy and the monastic order in Thailand.

The participants invited to the seminar in Isan included academics, specialists, local and national officials, and most important, the local villagers, as well as students and activists. This was the kind of dialogue-based event that Sulak and others were promoting in the period following the 14 October uprising, to let the voice of the grass roots be heard. This approach to addressing the country's many challenges was completely innovative and novel. Villagers had never been given a forum in which to speak directly to a government official from Bangkok. Dr. Puey and others reminded the gathering, especially the villagers, that this was what democracy brought—the opportunity to include all voices in participatory decision-making.

The region where the Pha Mong Dam was proposed was also home to a few thousand Communist insurgents. It was a tense political atmosphere in this part of Isan, and the villagers had little reason to trust Communists, democrats, students, or government workers. Villagers were simply trying to provide for their families. But for the last twenty years they had been harassed by Thai and Lao Communist guerrillas on both sides of the Mekong, by oppressive government directives and bribery, and by new massive development schemes like the proposed dam, mining, logging, and extensive pesticide spraying for agribusiness's monocrops.

A video cameraman and crew accompanied the organizers to document the experience of the villagers at the seminar. One of the villagers who offered testimony about the effects of the Mekong dams was thirty-year-old Tongpan. The docudrama film would eventually be named after him. Tongpan and his family had already been displaced by a dam elsewhere, and he had recently been laid off from his night shift at a sawmill that illegally logged timber. His was a precarious existence, and his wife and three children often went hungry. Tongpan was a typical example of the down-and-out, illiterate villagers to whom Sulak was seeking to give voice—and exactly the kind of Siamese from whom Sulak was learning about local realities.

Sulak himself was featured in *Tongpan*, which was released in 1977. His finely tailored white Nehru-collared jacket contrasted sharply with the worn-out cotton T-shirts of the villagers and the khaki safari wear of the academics. Sulak spoke sharply at the seminar, using the proposed dam as a microcosm for the main problem in the country. With his fire-and-brimstone manner and rhetoric, he could have been mistakenly perceived as talking down to the people. But Sulak intended to empower villagers like Tongpan with a new sense of independence, critical thinking, and a freedom to speak about their experience.

"We are always told to believe the experts, especially if they are *farang*, or [white] foreigners," Sulak says in the film while pointing at a British hydrologist who praised the damming of the Mekong with statistics and charts that were incomprehensible to the villagers. "They want to make Siam like the West.... What's the use? So-called development only serves a few politicians in Bangkok. Do we see the advantage of electricity here? Electricity brings radios and TVs that tell people to buy things. The *farang* industries get richer, but what about the destruction of our country? The whole province of Loei will be flooded by this Pha Mong Dam. People will be homeless and temples destroyed, and the giant *buk* fish, unique to the Mekong, breeds right where they are going to build the dam. The *buk* will be extinct. Are these *farang* interested? Or are the people in Bangkok concerned?"

By all accounts, Sulak was decades ahead of his time in his concern about and protest of modern development, particularly international development policies and practices. He would repeat for decades his call for Thailand and other Southeast Asian countries to reject the development models coming from America, the World Bank, the International Monetary Fund, and Japan, all of which, he argued, always focused on increased productivity, resource extraction, and profit. Sulak characterized these development models as an updated version of colonialism because the benefits of productivity remained with the political elite and corporations. He also rejected outright the ultraleft and Communist promise of a workers' utopia. Instead, Sulak wanted a Siamese resurgence of village-based cooperation where economics were practiced "as if people mattered." In the 1980s, using E. F. Schumacher's *Small Is Beautiful* as a blueprint, Sulak fully articulated his vision of a Buddhist development and an economic system where the ultimate aim was not production or increase of quantity or quality, but rather the contentment of individuals, arrived at by reducing the craving for material gain altogether.

But that was yet to come. Now, in the mid-1970s, Sulak was still watching the Western models of "development of the Third World" unfold in his region, and he was critical at every stage in his essays, speeches, and seminars.

There was an unexpected and shocking end to the seminar in Isan, which the film crew happened to document. When Tongpan returned by bus to his wife and family, his son was waiting along the roadside. The five-year-old boy said stoically, "Mama died." As Tongpan hastened home with his son in his arms, the boy added, "And she never got the water buffalo that you promised her."

Tongpan and his wife had been employed by the local government to spray the chemical pesticide DDT. It was the only work they could find in the shantytown they moved to after relocating their home. While

The photograph of Dr. Puey (*standing far right*), Sulak
(*kneeling second from left*), Stewart Meacham (*standing third
from right*), and others that was published in right-wing
periodicals, falsely claimed to show members of the
Communist Party of Thailand. The photo was taken after a
seminar about the Pha Mong Dam project.

Tongpan had been at the seminar, his wife had been exposed to a high dose of DDT and died instantaneously of acute pesticide exposure.

Sulak and the film crew sponsored the funerary rites for Tongpan's wife. The incident was seen by many as a tragically ironic confirmation of Sulak's opposition to Western development.

On the last day of the three-day seminar, a group photograph was snapped, showing three dozen people, all smiling and relaxed. Within a few days, it appeared in *Dao Siam*, a right-wing newspaper, and the *Bangkok Post*, which was controlled by the military at the time. *Dao Siam* published the photograph as proof that a "secret meeting" of the Communist Party of Isan had recently been held. Dr. Puey's face was circled, as were Sulak's and Meacham's. Dr. Puey was highlighted as the chairman, and Sulak was identified as a leading member of the CPT. The American Meacham was singled out as a Russian KGB agent. The charge of being a Communist was nothing to ignore, and Dr. Puey and Sulak were forced to defend themselves in the press.

"I was often accused of being a Communist by the military and by right-wing extremists like the Village Scouts," Sulak says. "Simultaneously, left-wing activists accused me of being a CIA agent and in the pocket of the Americans." One of the reasons why he was accused of being a US spy was that it became public knowledge that the funding sources of the *Social Science Review* originated from America's CIA. "When a monk goes out on alms rounds, does he ask, 'Is this food from a robber, or did you steal this food?'?" Sulak asks with a slight smile. "No, the monk just accepts the food. I was the same. Besides, maybe we could clean up some of the US's sins!"

In early 1976, Sulak and a number of Buddhist abbots, Catholics, Protestant members of the Church of Christ in Thailand, and Muslims met to discuss the increasing violence between the left and right political wings. The result of this meeting was the founding of the Coordinating Group for Religion in Society (CGRS). Sulak appointed two of his closest acolytes, Wisit Wangwinyu and Paisal Wongworawisit (later known by the monastic name Paisan), as the co-directors, and an office was set up to document and catalogue the human rights violations by government, right-wing militants, and Communists in Thailand, including disappearances, tortures, and murders. CGRS published its findings in *Human Rights in Thailand*, sharing the information with worldwide organizations such as Amnesty International. CGRS also began to give trainings in Bangkok and around the country on nonviolence and social action, offered legal aid to the poor and displaced, and provided civil rights education. Sulak was active in advising workers and raising funds from Christian missionaries for the work. Although human rights organizations like CGRS were allowed to function, many in the military did not appreciate the transparency they were trying to bring to society.

After 14 October 1973, Sulak's home continued to bustle with new arrivals of activists, politicians, artists, and international peace promoters. Poverty-stricken farmers and struggling musicians sometimes appeared at his doorstep, and Sulak often gave them money out of his own wallet. Political dissidents from Burma, Cambodia, Sri Lanka, and elsewhere slept in a spare bedroom.

And always present at his home were the fresh faces of students, his acolytes, each with his own kind of apprenticeship under Sulak. By the mid-1970s, there were two generations of acolytes. The most prominent of the first generation were, as Sulak's calls them, the "Gang of Four"— Pibhop Dhongchai, Thepsiri Sooksopa, Uthai Dulyakasem, and Vichai Chokevivat—who had formed the core of the Suksit Siam discussion group. The most prominent of the second generation of acolytes included Wisit Wangwinyu, Pracha Hutanuwatr, Santisuk Sophonsiri, and Paisal Wongworawisit. These two generations of acolytes, and others, were working with the Sathirakoses-Nagapradipa Foundation, the Komol Keemthong Foundation, CGRS, and other projects in Sulak's orbit.

"We came to Sulak from many different social, educational, and financial backgrounds, but we all had one overriding concern," Santisuk Sophonsiri recalls. "We were trying to find answers to the crisis in Thai society."

Of the hundreds of students who came to Sulak, some remained for a short time, either because they quickly gleaned from Sulak what they needed or because they felt him to be too abrasive. Sulak was rarely gentle, but he was always generous. His circle of acolytes was mostly male, and Sulak admits that the kind of camaraderie he cultivated had male chauvinistic tendencies. Sulak has always promoted equal treatment of women, but he has not always demonstrated it. Some found Sulak to be dismissive of women, but there were female acolytes anyway, including Rosana Tositrakul.

Sulak did not cultivate any kind of cult of personality around him, as did other Ajahns, such as Kukrit Pramoj. What the students saw was exactly what they got—a man who was direct and plainspoken—even brutally frank and harsh sometimes—and nearly always impatient. He was an inspiring figure, speaking to the ideals of dreamers and students and those who wanted to change the world. And Sulak was continually introducing his students to new ideas and individuals—including Dr. A. T. Ariyaratne and the Sarvodaya Movement, to whom Sulak sent his Gang of Four in 1970; Thich Nhat Hanh, whom Sulak brought to Thailand to meet his students in 1975 and afterward; the Quakers and Peace Brigade International, to whom Sulak sent students in the 1980s; and

Tibetan Buddhist teachers, including the Dalai Lama, of whom Sulak became the strongest supporter in Thailand. From the time of the founding of the *Review* in the late 1960s, through his work with the grass roots in the 1970s, to the establishment of many NGOs in the 1980s, Sulak's boundless energy and dynamism were supported and enabled by the many acolytes around him, and he in turn empowered them. Sulak thrived on their vigor, and they turned to Sulak for his worldly wisdom and advice.

Many of Sulak's acolytes gained their own platform for their future careers. To name just a few: Pibhop Dhongchai opened the first alternative school in Thailand, the Children's Village School, with his wife, Rajani Dhongchai, and became a leader in the Yellow Shirts political movement. Vichai became a renowned medical doctor. Uthai became president of Silpakorn University. Thepsiri became an avant-garde artist in Thailand. Sanpasit Kumprapan became known worldwide for his children's rights activism, including campaigns against child labor and child prostitution. Rosana was elected to the Thai senate in 2006. And the peripatetic monk Phra Paisal Visalo (the monastic name of Paisal Wongworawisit), cofounded Sekiyadhamma, an organization that supports the work of socially engaged monks and nuns throughout Thailand.

"I can claim some credit for many of my students who have become important to society," Sulak says. "They offer something alternative to the mainstream, either in Dhamma, socialism, spirituality, or for the environment. . . . I did play an important role for them in the beginning. Perhaps this is my ego, but I feel as though I started to grow them from seeds."

Yet, among the many acolytes who remained for an extended period and worked closely with Sulak—editing or writing for one of his journals, working for the many NGOs he established, traveling with him to work on projects in the jungles or villages, or attending to his personal affairs at Suksit Siam, at Klett Thai, or at his home—there are very few who did not leave Sulak at some point in frustration, anger, or discontent. Sulak admits that he even "chucked a few of my students out" when he thought circumstances required it, either because they were financially deceptive or because Sulak thought the student needed to strike out on his own. While Sulak appreciated having many students around him to help with the enormous workload, he still did not try to reel any of the students back in if they left disillusioned or disgruntled.

There were a variety of reasons why students left their work with Sulak, but most often it was due to his being overbearing, critical, and impatient. Even his closest students, including the Gang of Four as well as Pracha, Wisit, and others, decided to break with Sulak for a time. There have always been new students to fill the work void left when senior acolytes departed. But inevitably, nearly every former follower came back to Sulak, sometimes within months, sometimes after decades, to reconcile. Even those who were once very close to Sulak and left in anger reengage with him after time dissolved the friction. And while they may not return to work directly for Sulak or one of his many projects, they still offer a respectful bow and bring a bottle of wine for their teacher. As the community activist Jane Rasbash has said, "Once you are in Sulak's circle, you can never really fall out of it."

"It is actually a compliment to Sulak that he doesn't have any completely submissive disciples," Prof. Nidhi said. "Almost all of his disciples deviate from him, rebel against him from time to time. This is actually Sulak's strength. Most [Ajahns] in Thailand dominate too much. But not Sulak."

By mid-1976, Thailand's political atmosphere was unpredictable. The Thai military and King were extremely nervous because they saw Communist insurgents overthrowing other governments in the region. The King and generals had aligned themselves with the right-wing elements in the country. When South Vietnam fell to the Viet Cong in April 1975, the US military soon pulled out of Thailand. Just weeks before Saigon fell, the Khmer Rouge captured the Cambodian capital, Phnom Penh, and Pol Pot began his reign of terror southeast of Thailand. By the end of the year, the Communist Party of Laos had overthrown the government, sending the Laotian king and queen and other members of the royal family to "reeducation" camps, where most of them died. The Thai royal family had deep familial and historical links with the royal neighbors, and King Bhumibol could have easily imagined insurgents in his own country trying to dethrone him. Knowing the fate of the Laos royals, the King was more uneasy than ever and, fearing a volatile situation, allowed a heavy authoritarian hand in his own country. Already the palace was supporting Nawaphon, a secretive right-wing nationalist group of individuals from the military, government, business world, and Buddhist hierarchy that fostered antileftist and antistudent agitation. Additionally, by 1975, the workers' strikes and student protests in Thailand threatened the stable and growing economy, which directly threatened the economic interests of the Thai royal family.

The specter of a Communist takeover of Thailand sent the Village Scouts and Red Gaurs into frenzied hunts for sympathizers, which sometimes resulted in extrajudicial killings and the bombing of suspected gatherings of leftists. The liberalization of the media since 1973 unleashed ultranationalist radio and television programs that brought paranoia into people's homes with slogans like "Right Kill Left!" and suggestions that

Sulak Sivaraksa and the Path of Socially Engaged Buddhism

Buddhism condoned the killing of any Communist. All the while, students, workers, and the progressive left pushed back against the right-wing reactionary forces. They hoped that there would still be new intellectual freedom, civil liberties, and workers' rights enshrined into law—all of which the right wing saw as a conspiracy against their "Nation, Religion, and Monarchy."

The Thai military was ready to reassert the control they had ceded in 1973 to civilian rule. The previous dictator, Thanom, and his two cronies, Colonel Narong and General Praphas, were invited by the military to return from exile to Thailand. Thanom knew that he would be unwelcome to a great many Thai, so after sneaking into the country, he disguised himself in the robes of an ordained Buddhist monk, a time-honored evasive technique in Thai politics, which usually provided protection for a short period. He was allowed to take up monastic residence at the Buddhist temple most closely associated with the throne, where the King himself had been a monk. Soon the second of the tyrants, General Praphas, also slipped back into the country, saying that he needed medical treatment for his heart.

"This was the first time I was angry with the King," Sulak admits. "It was when the King not only allowed Thanom back to Siam after exile, but he even permitted the crook to be ordained in a royal temple. This was a disgrace."

Protests broke out across Bangkok against the return of Thanom and his henchman Praphas. Even with the protests, the King and Queen visited Thanom at the temple to show their support for him. After two labor activists who had been putting up protest signs west of Bangkok were lynched and their bodies hung on a wall, the National Student Center of Thailand, along with other students and the National Labor Council of Thailand, joined the growing demonstration. They called for

Right-wing mobs lynched students during the 6 October
1976 massacre at Thammasat University.

the arrest of those responsible for the lynching and demanded that Thanom be expelled from the country. On 4 October, more than 2,000 students and workers gathered at Thammasat University to discuss their next steps. As part of the protest program, a mock demonstration of the lynching was staged. The next day, *Dao Siam* published a photograph of the demonstration, with a caption saying that the student in the mock hanging bore a resemblance to the Crown Prince, Vajiralongkorn. Additional accusations of lèse-majesté against the student protesters were asserted by others in the right wing. The Nawaphon, the Village Scouts, and the Red Gaurs piled on, accusing all the student protesters of defaming the monarchy and of being Communists. It was reason enough to attack. Astonishingly, King Bhumibol agreed with the lèse-majesté accusations, and 4,000 military, paramilitary, and police troops were deployed to Thammasat University to crush the student and worker protest. Another thousand right-wing vigilantes were at the ready with guns and clubs.

Thailand's three-year experiment with democracy came to an end the next day, on 6 October 1976. If 14 October 1973 was the darkest day in Thai history, then 6 October 1976 surely would be its bloodiest.

At 5:30 a.m. on 6 October, after the exits to the university were blocked, army snipers and police opened fire on the students and workers on the campus grounds. The shelling could be heard across the street in the Grand Palace, the spiritual center of Thailand and home of the royal family. Mayhem broke out. Screaming students ran in every direction. The student speaker on the podium pleaded over the loudspeaker to stop the bullets and grenades that were raining down. Bodies fell limp everywhere. Students pulled bullet-ridden bodies behind trees and tried to staunch the bleeding wounds. Other students were shot while attempting to crawl to safety. Some managed to climb the surrounding fence but were immediately shot and stomped to death by the vigilante mob. When a third of the students took refuge in the Commerce Studies building, antitank missiles were discharged at the structure. The Border Patrol Police then stormed the campus. Lynch mobs of Red Gaurs and Village Scouts, some with pistols, most with batons and chains, followed the police and beat students to death. Two corpses were hung on trees, and crowds clapped as eyes were gouged and the bodies beaten with metal rods. Across the street, in front of the Ministry of Justice, three people, alive but unconscious, were set upon a stack of tires, soaked with gasoline, and lit on fire. This massacre—captured on film and video—took the lives of over a hundred students and workers. Thousands were injured. The public spectacle of horror lasted until the midday. An estimated 3,000 students were arrested.

By late afternoon of 6 October, a navy admiral was appointed supreme commander of the newly established National Administrative Reform Council (NARC), which would head the government. King Bhumibol was briefed on all matters and approved the NARC leadership. The admiral announced over television and radio that NARC was needed to protect stability, to defend the Thai monarchy, and to prevent a Vietnamese-sponsored Communist takeover of Thailand.

Baker and Phongpaichit declare in *A History of Thailand*, "With 6 October 1976, the military and its allies had shot and bombed urban radicalism into submission. But the awfulness of the Thammasat massacre was a profound social shock that ensured it marked a new beginning as well as a terrible conclusion."

In Sulak's mind, the institution of the monarchy and King Bhumibol had always been inseparable. But with the involvement of King Bhumibol in the massacre, Sulak recognized the deeply flawed character of this particular king. It was at this time that he separated the man from the institution.

"This became the turning point for me with the King. This King knew of the whole bloody thing," Sulak said.

....

Sulak addressing the Assembly of the Poor in Ubon Rajadhani.

Chapter 6

Seeds of Peace

Sulak was not in Thailand during the Thammasat University massacre of 6 October 1976. He had been invited to the United States for the 1976 Bicentennial celebration in July at the Smithsonian Institution. He represented his country at the Smithsonian despite a protest from the US ambassador in Thailand, who objected to Sulak's criticism of American foreign policy in Southeast Asia, in particular Vietnam.

On his return to Bangkok in early October, Sulak stopped in the UK to stay with his half-brother in London. During dinner an urgent telegram arrived from Sulak's wife telling him not to return to Thailand. It was too dangerous. Sulak immediately went to find a copy of the *London Evening News*. An article about the massacre and violence featured a photograph of a student hanging from a rope on a tree and being beaten by a right-wing mob at Thammasat University, one of several such barbarities that occurred on 6 October. And he read in the *Times of London* about his arrest in absentia for treason. Knowing that progressive writers, publishers, thinkers, students, and activists were arrested, Sulak was distressed, yet he could not return home, out of fear for his life.

While in London, Sulak learned that police ransacked and then shuttered the doors of the Suksit Siam bookstore and Klett Thai publishing house, and confiscated thousands of books. With two tanks, the military blocked the lane to Sulak's house and the Komol Keemthong Foundation office located in a nearby building. Nilchawee was taken into the police station by paramilitary for questioning; she was released unharmed. "She was very brave," Sulak recalls. "She said she alone was responsible for the Foundation's office." But the generals knew who they were looking for—Sulak. The military allowed a television crew into the Foundation's second-floor office to show the alleged national headquarters of the Communist Party of Thailand. Sulak was again accused of being a Communist. "They would have killed me," he says.

Three truckloads of books from the Komol Keemthong Foundation, as well as all the publications from the Sathirakoses-Nagapradipa Foundation, numbered at more than 200,000, were taken and burned.

Sulak immediately contacted Dr. Puey, who had evaded the mobs and military after the 6 October massacre. American and German diplomats helped Dr. Puey escape the country, and he was safe in Germany. He was at the top of the government's long list of people associated with the students whom the military was arresting on the trumped-up charges of being Communist sympathizers. Dr. Puey soon came to London, where he and Sulak set up the Mitra Thai (Friends of Thai) Trust to collect funds to send back to Thailand for aid in paying the legal fees of those arrested, and to publicize the atrocities in Thailand. They traveled across Europe and North America together to brief members of European parliaments and the US Congress; to speak at universities, associations, and groups; and to meet with Thai living abroad to discuss the dire situation. The Mitra Thai Trust also published a monthly newspaper in London. Sulak arranged for a Thai Airways flight attendant to smuggle copies back into Thailand. They secretly communicated with Nicholas Bennett and those at the Coordinating Group for Religion in Society in Bangkok.

"The Thai government was saying Ajahn Puey and Ajahn Sulak were very dangerous because they were afraid that they would incite more student unrest," Arkom Tulardilok said. Arkom is a Thai criminologist who was studying for his PhD in the US at the time. Many Thai living abroad, including students, wanted Dr. Puey and Sulak to establish a government in exile, which they both rejected. Instead their focus was on mobilizing international support to pressure the military junta to lift martial law, release the imprisoned, and return the power to the people according to the most recent constitution. Arkom hosted Dr. Puey and Sulak at Michigan State University in Lansing. "Puey just wanted to inform politicians with facts in every country. Sulak instead wanted to make people act," he said. "Same goal but they had different methods." Arkom recalls seeing Sulak in his living room meditating in the mornings and evenings "to cool down his mind."

When Sulak was not traveling in late 1976, he stayed in England at the home of old friends he had met at Lampeter College. Still, Sulak faced financial hardship and was grateful to receive support from the International Association for Cultural Freedom. He used the time to restart the yoga posture practice that he had begun in 1969 in Bangkok under the tutelage of Josephine Stanton, the wife of the former US ambassador to Thailand, Edwin F. Stanton.

In December of 1976 Sulak traveled to France to meet the exiled Vietnamese Buddhist teacher Thich Nhat Hanh, who was living outside

Paris at the Sweet Potato Farm community he had founded after his exile from Vietnam. The two had met in 1972 at an interfaith gathering in Sri Lanka, and Sulak invited him to Thailand in 1975 to interact with and teach students. Sulak was deeply inspired by the Zen monk's commitment to both social engagement and meditation practice. Thay (or "Teacher," as Thich Nhat Hanh is often called) taught Sulak meditation techniques, principally mindfulness of breathing, among other practices.

"Drinking tea, I wanted to talk, but he always encouraged me to be silent and mindful of holding the cup, drinking the tea—a kind of mindfulness in the moment," Sulak says. Thich Nhat Hanh's instructions became part of Sulak's lifelong meditation practice. "For Thay, his meditation practice has been constant his whole life. Mine is always on and off. But I try. I use it more to calm my angry mind."

With the military firmly in charge in Thailand in 1976, there was no hope in sight for Sulak's safe return. While it caused Sulak distress to be away from his family and colleagues, he relished being identified by the Thai government as a public enemy. He used his political exile to build his global network and increase his profile as a preeminent Buddhist advocate for peace, justice, and civil rights as well as a Siamese scholar. Sulak's reputation was bolstered by the unified call for nonviolence that emerged in the 1980s among other prominent Buddhists, including Thich Nhat Hanh, Maha Ghosananda, the Dalai Lama, and Aung San Su Kyi. Sulak's varied work and personal interaction with these leaders shaped his articulation of a socially engaged Buddhism. Among academics and Buddhist activists in the West, Sulak's name became synonymous with socially engaged Buddhism, which was the platform that he used to

Opposite page: Nilchawee, Khwan, Sulak, Ming, and Chim at their traditional teak home in Bangkok.

establish his international reputation. Indeed, Sulak's intellectual acumen and rebellious reputation became more appreciated internationally than in Thailand, especially after 1976.

Prof. Herbert Phillips arranged a visiting professorship for Sulak at the University of California, Berkeley, in 1977. With support from the Ford and Rockefeller foundations, Sulak moved to Berkeley. Support from the American Friends Service Committee enabled Sulak's family— Nilchawee and their son and first daughter, Chim and Khwan—to join him in exile. Chim had been studying at Assumption College in Bangkok, where he was mocked by other students for being "the son of a Communist." He had a difficult time dealing with his father's status as persona non grata, accused of treason, and pilloried in the press. It was a relief for Chim to leave behind the ridicule he'd endured in Thailand.

Sulak taught Buddhism and Southeast Asian history at Berkeley, meditated with students on campus and in the nearby redwood forests, took them on field trips to Zen centers, and invited them to his home for Nilchawee's spicy noodles. He loved the youthful enthusiasm of his students and thrived emotionally on their eagerness to work with a bona fide political dissident.

After six months in California, Nilchawee returned home with Khwan. Chim remained with Sulak. Sulak took various short-term teaching posts, moving to Cornell University, Michigan State University, and the University of Hawai'i. In Hawai'i, Sulak met Prof. David W. Chappell, founder of the Society for Buddhist-Christian Studies. They collaborated on a number of writing projects, and Chappell later edited the Festschrift *Socially Engaged Spirituality: Essays in Honor of Sulak Sivaraksa on His Seventieth Birthday* (2003). Sulak called Chappell (who died in 2004) "my best friend in the West." For the peripatetic Siamese, calling the professor his best friend was a unique acknowledgment;

despite his many friends around the world, very few actually came to know Sulak's emotional side as Chappell did. He saw Sulak work with students in both the United States and Thailand, and wrote in Sulak's book *A Buddhist Vision for Renewing Society* (1981): "He refuses to be swept away by any movement, whether it be economic, ideological, moral or political, which neglects or is unfair to some segment of society. A supporter of the young, he understands but avoids their rhetoric, and rejects their call for revolution. On the other hand, he refuses to stand still and accept the status quo when it demeans or oppresses others. Idealistic, active and vocal, against injustice, he has often seemed offensive."

Sulak's exiles from Thailand, the first in 1976–1977 and the second in 1991–1994, were periods marked by the outward expression of his views rather than times for internal reflection. Sulak was never a contemplative in a spiritual sense, and he certainly did not lean toward the mystical. Sulak's daily meditation practice, using Thich Nhat Hanh's instructions and his prayers in Pali, was more an antidote to dampen frustration than a means of transcendence. Though his exiles could have been a time for extended spiritual retreat, Sulak chose the life of a busy activist-professor. The calm path of a studious sage was not Sulak's calling.

Sulak's choice to participate in intellectual and political spheres during exile was not only because of the prevailing circumstances, acute though they were. Sulak needed constant interaction with the public because of his discomfort with facing his deepest fear—loneliness. He needed to bounce his ideas off people in classrooms and rallies and discussion groups; he wanted to see if his concepts and views gained traction in the hearts and minds of students and youth. Sulak's public role gave him deep satisfaction. He was not one to silently consider his thoughts, letting the inevitable loneliness arise and pass as he reviewed his past actions and where the future might take him. Rather, Sulak created in America, as he had in Thailand, a place for himself to be an energetic hub. There was a reciprocal relationship between Sulak and the students with whom he surrounded himself: he inspired them with practical wisdom, and they in turn provided him with the comfort and solace he needed. Whether at home or abroad, Sulak consistently maintained the public image of a strong man, a tireless campaigner for justice, and someone who could always be counted on to speak truth to power. His vulnerabilities are difficult to see in his public face, and he doesn't speak to anyone about what seemingly troubles him most—his fear of isolation, fading from importance, and being forgotten.

The historian David Streckfuss believes that Sulak is more concerned about what people think about his ideas than about him as a person: "Sulak wants to be recognized. But it's because he wants his ideas heard and considered carefully. Yes, he is an intellectual, but in my mind Sulak is an activist. Ideas have power. And they have the possibility of action; they inspire action. Ideas give you heart to continue on, they give meaning. This is an important element of Sulak's activism."

Sulak's exile brought him into closer touch with the American Quaker community. While the monks Buddhadasa and Payutto prepared his intellect for socially engaged Buddhism, it was the Quakers who gave Sulak tools for nonviolent social action. Sulak knew the Quakers well, having worked with them in Southeast Asia in the early 1970s. He had invited his Quaker friends George and Lillian Willoughby to Thailand in 1974 to lead workshops on nonviolence. Sulak says, "It was really the Quakers who paved the way for me to make all of my connections throughout East and Southeast Asia." With the support of Quakers, he traveled throughout the region, meeting many of the leading intellectuals, religious leaders, and activists. Brewster Grace of the American Friends Service Committee in Singapore had financed Sulak's first travels around the region in 1973–1974. Sulak had no previous firsthand experience in Japan, Vietnam, Indonesia, Burma, Singapore, Malaysia, or the Philippines.

Sulak had kept in close touch with his Quaker friends, and while he was teaching at Berkeley, they invited him to Mexico in July 1977 to attend the International Seminar on Training for Nonviolent Action. Sulak and his acolyte Paisal traveled to the popular resort city of Cuernavaca to attend the three-week training.

Meeting the Quakers in Mexico had an impact on Sulak that was not unlike his encounter a decade earlier with Prince Sitthiporn. The Prince opened Sulak's eyes to his own shortcomings—that he was too much of an intellectual elitist. If Sulak wanted to help his countrymen, the Prince told him, he needed to go into the villages and countryside to meet suffering face to face. Seeing the Quakers in Mexico was also a wakeup call for Sulak. If Sulak really wanted to bring about change in society, the Quakers told him, he needed to directly confront state power. George Lakey and the Willoughbys, with their Movement for a New Society, inspired Sulak. They spoke passionately about the need to decentralize political power and about ways to resist authority. In the 1980s, Sulak sent some of own students to work with Peace Brigades International, founded by a group of peace activists including George Willoughby.

"I found the Quakers to be even more articulate than Buddhists on why we need to question and resist the powers of the state," Sulak told Donald Rothberg, a Buddhist teacher of socially engaged spirituality, in 1993. "If the state supports violence, we must resist. Buddhists in my country and elsewhere have for too long coexisted with nation-states that perpetuate violence."

The discussions that Sulak had with the Quakers, as well as

various Christian social activists, helped him to see the link between many of the worldwide societal maladies of the twentieth century. The maverick Catholic priest and social critic Ivan Illich, whom Sulak met at the gathering in Mexico, helped mold Sulak's views on the connection between modern education and poverty. Illich's *Deschooling Society* (1971) and other works were blueprints for the alternative schools Sulak and his disciples would later establish in Thailand, Burma, Laos, and Cambodia, under the auspices of the Spirit in Education Movement (SEM), founded by Sulak in 1995.

Sulak had identified critical problems in his country in the late 1960s, including the uprooting of people from traditional culture and religion, failure to teach critical thinking in schools, and pervasive consumerism and capitalism, which encourage people to look for contentment in products rather than within themselves. While he had not yet found clear solutions, he knew that education was key. It was Illich, and also Sulak's reading of Paolo Freire, the Brazilian philosopher, educator, and author of the classic *Pedagogy of the Oppressed* (English edition, 1970), that stimulated Sulak to examine critically how the failures of modern education have led societies toward a more impoverished state, both materially and spiritually.

Sulak's observations in Thailand and Southeast Asia were confirmed by Illich's *Deschooling Society*. "School introduces youth into a world in which everything can be measured, including their imagination and even their own selves," Illich writes. "School prepares people for the alienating institutionalization of life, by teaching the necessity of being taught. Once this lesson is learned, people lose their incentive to develop independently; they no longer find it attractive to relate to each other, and the surprises that life offers when it is not predetermined by institutional definition are closed." Sulak was fond of quoting Illich's statement that schools, whether in America, the UK, or Thailand, were "the advertising agency which makes you believe that you need the society as it is." He had come away from his three weeks with the Quakers inspired to bring to his message a clearer presentation of nonviolence and a radically different vision of educational pedagogy.

It was at this time in the late 1970s that Sulak began to reconsider the efficacy of having social movements led by charismatic individuals rather than by a group. "Gandhi insisted on the power of truth—*satyagraha*—and it mobilized a huge portion of the Indian population against the powerful British Empire. He used the truth and *ahimsa*—nonviolence—to empower the poor and illiterate," Sulak says. "Gandhi was a success. But he also failed in some respects because it was a one-man show." Observing the Quakers, Sulak began to advocate for decentralized leadership, whether for a small organizations or a large social movement.

"Social action and movements need a body of individuals, a community, to have seeds of peace within them, not only the inspiring leader who embodies nonviolence. Having nonviolence inside a group, we develop loving-kindness, and learn how not to hate our oppressors, even while we work together to deconstruct the oppressive system. This is more powerful when it is a led by a group and not a single person."

Before Sulak left Mexico, he had expressed his gratitude to his Quaker friends with these words: "What I like about you is that you remain small, you don't missionize your philosophy, and how you all have such a good sense of humor and make fun of yourselves. The world is better off because of you Quakers."

Tensions eased in Thailand in late 1977 while Sulak was still teaching in the United States. Another coup placed General Kriangsak Chomanand in power. Kriangsak was a lifelong soldier who was more open to democracy than most senior military men at the time. When he became prime minister, Kriangsak granted amnesty to political dissidents, including Sulak. With his arrest in absentia dropped, Sulak returned home in 1978, after eighteen months in exile.

Before leaving the States, Sulak compiled three different English manuscripts for books, which were subsequently published in Thailand. His most salient writings from the *Social Science Review* were translated and published as *Siam in Crisis* (1980). *A Buddhist Vision for Renewing Society*, which included his speeches and writings from exile, was issued in 1981. And lectures he gave in 1976, just before the military took over in Thailand, and writings in the early 1980s were collected in *Religion and Development* (1987). These were Sulak's first books in English, and established the format for his many books published in the future, most of which have benefited from the editorial and writing talents of native English-speakers such as Arnold Kotler, Nicholas Bennett, David Arnott, Alan Senauke, David Chappell, Jonathan Watts, and Jane Rasbash. Sulak's books, both in English and Thai, were most often a collection of speeches and articles on a wide range of political, social, and historical topics rather than in-depth studies of singular subjects. One of his foundations or organizations was usually the named publisher for Sulak's books—in Thai and in English—and the money made from the sales went directly to the organization's projects. The writings that Sulak has published mirror his character and message—hard-hitting with the intent of far-reaching goals, inspiring but challenging to implement, consistently resisting political and economic injustice, and calling out the hypocrisy of religious authorities.

Sulak's reputation in the United States and Europe had grown in the late 1970s, and he found a ready audience for his message. But, as David Chappell wrote in *A Buddhist Vision for Renewing Society*, "In

Sulak Sivaraksa and the Path of Socially Engaged Buddhism

Western circles Sulak is a delight . . . however, his reputation in Siam is somewhat different." Chappell quotes the following description of Sulak from an article in the *Bangkok Bank Monthly Review* (December 1975):

> Sulak Sivaraksa is a barrister-at-law, publisher, critic, lecturer, traditionalist—and thoroughly unpopular. Rightists call him an out-and-out Communist, while he disappoints the Leftists (and Rightist detractors) by rejecting Communism and most aspects of doctrinaire socialism. His position forms an eye of quiet, of common-sense wisdom, in the midst of the intellectual storm now raging. His very unpopularity is a recommendation to be listened to. He presents no ideal solutions, but his thought is wide enough to contain the best in tradition with the best in progressive thinking.

Even though some writers and editors in Thailand, like those at the *Bangkok Bank Monthly Review*, appreciated the complex character of Sulak, the authorities in Thailand were not so keen to embrace him. So when Sulak returned home in 1978, he had to be cautious. Some of his students and colleagues were in jail, and many had fled to the jungle, including Seksan Prasertkul, who became a leader in the Communist Party of Thailand. Sulak's rising intellectual star had faded. He was no longer invited to teach at the major universities. His publishing house and magazines had been shut down, and in his absence the Komol Keemthong and Sathirakoses-Nagapradipa foundations were struggling. The other NGOs he had initiated had little or no funding.

Sulak knew he had to begin again, and he decided to start where he always did—finding ways for his ideas to appear in print. He resurrected Klett Thai in 1978 under a new name—Kled Thai—because his

German benefactors, Klett Verlag, had withdrawn their support owing to Thailand's political volatility. Sulak also began to look for like-minded Catholics, Protestants, and other Christian organizations to engage in interfaith dialogues and discuss cooperation in development programs. Sulak's principal work in the 1980s emerged with his creation of models for social and economic development, especially those informed by religion, which were alternatives to the government model.

"I thought that the government and existing NGOs in the 1970s had failed because they did not work closely enough with the Buddhist monks. I wanted the monks to be aware of their power, to work with the grass roots, and not to obey the central Buddhist hierarchy, because it had become hopelessly corrupt."

Sulak wanted to bring a Buddhist paradigm into development, not only in Thailand but in Southeast Asia. Sulak's articulation was an updated version of Payutto's and Buddhadasa's work stressing that development should be measured not merely in material wealth but also in spiritual progress. In *Siamese Resurgence* (1985), Sulak stated, "From a Buddhist point of view, development must aim at the reduction of craving, the avoidance of violence, and the development of the spirit rather than of material things. As each individual progresses, he increasingly helps others without waiting for the millennium, or for the ideal socialist society."

In *A Buddhist Vision for Renewing Society*, he charged that "planners, as a whole, whether in the East or the West, do not want to take the time to study the complicated programs having to do with the ultimate goals of humanity. They excuse themselves by saying it is a problem of metaphysics or of religion, as though ultimate goals are beyond the ability of common people to understand." Sulak highlighted problems in specific programs of the World Bank and the International Monetary Fund and development aid programs by the United States, Japan, and others. It was a lost opportunity, in Sulak's view, not to use development as a vehicle for spiritual liberation, in addition to improving livelihoods and social conditions.

In the 1980s, Sulak became more interested in bringing harmony across religious traditions and national borders by working with different religious leaders. "Though we come from different religious traditions," Sulak wrote in his English memoir, "we take a similar stand on social issues and our work for peace. We are committed to our own tradition, but we are on the fringe and want to radicalize the tradition." He continued to integrate into his work the ideas he had gathered in exile, especially those of the Quakers and leading Roman Catholic figures such as Freire and Illich as well as Dorothy Day, Daniel and Philip Berrigan, Hans Küng, and Sulak's friend Tissa Balasuriya, a Sri Lankan theologian. Sulak was also studying and translating the writings of the American Trappist monk Thomas Merton. He had looked forward to meeting Merton, who had embarked on an exploration of Buddhist practice in Asia. Sadly, the day before their scheduled meeting in December 1968, Merton died in a tragic accident in his Bangkok hotel.

Sulak's Buddhist chauvinism had long since dissolved, and what emerged was an ecumenical attitude that believed cooperation among religious faiths was one of the principal means to transform society. Together with a small group of Catholic and Protestant friends in Bangkok, Sulak and his students—including Seri Phongphit, Wisit, and Phra Paisan Visalo—set up the Thai Inter-religious Commission for Development (TICD) in 1979, and initiated a magazine in Thai; in 1985 this periodical was changed into an English-language magazine called *Seeds of Peace*, a name given by Thich Nhat Hanh. In one of the first issues, Sulak wrote, "If we Buddhists want to play a meaningful role in reinstating the virtues of peace and justice in this world, we need to be bold enough to question the present violent and unjust structures, not only the single acts of individuals and countries. And, we will need to cooperate with Christians, Jews, Muslims and those of other religions and ideologies, asking questions like, 'Why are we so good at producing far too much and so bad at helping where there is too little?'"

Sulak also devoted time to the Asian Cultural Forum on Development (ACFOD), which he had been instrumental in launching in 1975. ACFOD continued while Sulak was in exile in 1976–1977. In 1981, after Sulak had returned to Thailand, he worked again for ACFOD, as coordinator for its programs, for seven years. Sulak not only raised money for ACFOD from international donors, but he was able to have ACFOD given consultative and liaison status within the United Nations. Sulak focused ACFOD's program efforts on poverty alleviation among fishermen, landless laborers, and working mothers in Southeast Asia. However, after Sulak clashed with some of ACFOD's senior staff, he resigned.

Sulak had held a dream of establishing an ashram, a spiritual community where he could promote cross-cultural understanding, interreligious dialogue, and meditation practice. He had long been inspired by intentional communities in India. While he wanted to preserve the contemplative aspect of most traditional ashrams, he also felt the need for a socially engaged element, incorporating debate to allow many different voices to be heard, as he had observed at the Aspen Institute in the United States, which he had visited in 1977, and among the Quakers. Sulak's dream was realized in 1984 when Ms. Saisawasdi Svasti contacted him and offered a plot of her family's land for a spiritual community, in honor of her late parents, Prince Suphasawadi Wongsanit and Samoh Svasti. The land was east of Bangkok in the Ongkharak

Sulak with some of his acolytes who lived at
Wongsanit Ashram.

District. Sulak called the community the Wongsanit Ashram in honor of the donors.

The quality of the land at Wongsanit Ashram was poor and had been contaminated by decades of pesticide use in cassava and pineapple cultivation. Sulak's students, almost all urban middle-class activists like Sulak himself, had idealized the rural life, but none had ever actually lived in a village, much less cultivated land. The handful of students struggled to grow their food in competition with insects and animals, including wild boars and monkeys, that consumed anything that sprouted. They lived in simple jungle dwellings, planted trees and shrubs, revived the soil with organic methods, and asked local villagers for help. Gradually they created a sustainable garden. The Heinrich Böll Foundation provided support in 1990 to redesign the land; build a community hall, simple dormitories, and a library; and improve the water system with a canal and ponds. A thriving community grew at the ashram, and they began to invite educators and social activists to lead programs in grassroots leadership, natural construction techniques, and empowerment of marginalized communities. The ashram continues to this day.

Sulak developed and raised the money for Wongsanit Ashram in the first year, and then, as with other projects, he turned the operation over to his students. This was Sulak's way in organizational development—sow the seeds and, after they take root, let others cultivate and gather the fruit. With the ashram up and running, in 1986 Sulak founded the Santi Pracha Dhamma Institute (Institute of Peace, Democracy, Truth, SPDI) in honor of Dr. Puey. Just as he later did with Pridi, Sulak wanted to honor the achievements of Dr. Puey, who was still living in exile in England since fleeing Thailand in 1976. Sulak wrote in his book *Puey Ungpakorn: An Honest Siamese in a Class of His Own* (2014) that "the powers that be wanted to expunge the good work of Puey Ungpakorn,

Sulak Sivaraksa and the Path of Socially Engaged Buddhism

whose influence was present in all fields. . . . I thought it would be a good idea to write about Puey, to make both his enemies and mine squirm, as they cannot bear to hear the truth." The Santi Pracha Dhamma Institute was immediately suspected by the military of being Puey's mouthpiece and was accused of treasonous activities such as supporting Communists. But Sulak skillfully managed to have the institute legally registered and guided it away from encounters with the authorities. It was soon hosting panel discussions and seminars on civil rights and democracy, conducting training in nonviolent social action, and producing training materials in Thai, Burmese, and English, for programs on sustainable village economics, appropriate technology, and alternatives to consumerism. The institute also became the liaison for the Assembly of the Poor, a grassroots organization that in the 1990s was a leading voice for marginalized communities.

Sulak had always been a networker, since his days as a student in England. His thick address book is a constant companion during his travels around the world. Business cards and scraps of papers covered with hasty scribbles inevitably fall out when he opens it. Sulak has a habit, upon arrival in a new place, of finding a friend's home or office and sitting with his address book for an hour or two, telephoning anyone in the area he knows, to schedule a meeting, to reconnect, to share news. Sulak is constantly communicating and connecting. Whenever international guests stay with Sulak at his home, after he fulfills his duties as a gracious host over long dinners with fine red wine, he sends his friends off with a bag of letters, postcards, and recent publications for them to post from their home country—Sulak uses every opportunity he can to save money, even at his friends' expense. Every New Year since the mid-1970s, Sulak has sent out over a thousand New Year cards personally signed, often along with the most recent *Seeds of Peace* issue or a copy of his latest book. Wherever he goes, in Thailand or abroad—from London to Los Angeles, from Mandalay to Stockholm, from Delhi to Berlin—Sulak is constantly connecting with friends. Dr. Kasean Techapeera, political science professor and 1976 student leader, wrote of Sulak, "He is a linker, selector, interactor, supervisor, demonstrator, dialoguer, discusser, and dialectician between different cultures, different discourses. His contribution as an innovator is to bring together people from different schools of thought and different systems to exchange ideas and search for mutual learning and understanding. Sulak can assume this role because he uses himself as a model of discourse mixing. He demonstrates the way to synthesize the left and the right, the old and the new."

Sulak seems to remember everyone he meets, and he reinforces his memory with constant communication. And it not just those he has met who he speaks about as if they were close friends. Talking with Sulak about history, literature, or politics, the first-time listener is astonished by the close immediacy with which Sulak speaks of individuals and relationships, often from centuries ago, as if knew them all personally.

Part of Sulak's power of recall comes not from remaining in deep states of meditation but rather from his morning habit of writing in his journal. He writes about the previous day—the names of people he met, the topic of discussion, the places visited, the books he just read, the lectures he attended, and all the various details of his day. And he writes about it every day—since he was fourteen years old. The exercise has led Sulak to have an incredible memory. "After I started writing in my diary as a boy, I haven't stopped, and now it is a habit," he reports. His journals fill over thirty volumes. Sulak and his longtime secretary, Ladda Wiwatsurawech, regularly consult them for specific details. Ladda is only person who can fully decipher Sulak's sprawling cursive in Thai; even he has difficulty rereading his own handwriting. Each year Sulak's younger daughter, Ming, has the journals bound in leather, and the volumes now fill a wall of bookshelves in his library. "It is no value, really!" Sulak insists. "Unlike Virginia Woolf's diary where she penetrates deeply. My diary is just no bloody use."

By the late 1980s, Sulak wanted to formalize his loose network of Buddhist friends and activists around the world into an organization that would enable them to coordinate, collaborate, and assist each other. There were large organizations such as the World Fellowship of Buddhists (WFB) that brought together Buddhists from around the world, but these were, as Sulak calls them, "Big *B* Buddhists." The distinction between "big *B* Buddhism" and "small *b* buddhism"—a contrast between Buddhism as a religion and the Dhamma as Truth itself—was an idea that Sulak first got from David Arnott, a specialist in human rights in Burma. According to Sulak, "Big *B* Buddhism" consists of mainstream groups that promote the status quo of institutionalized religion and its relationship with state power. This includes the WFB as well as the rigid monastic hierarchy in Theravada countries such as Thailand and Sri Lanka, or among very wealthy Buddhist schools in Japan, Korea, Taiwan, and elsewhere in Asia.

"Big *B* Buddhists are more concerned with building gilded temples than with understanding the Buddha's teachings. They use fancy and expensive rituals to serve their own purpose. Their concern should be for the poor, not their rich benefactors. We must see how the materialism of Big *B* Buddhism is part of the problem!"

In 1989, Sulak and Pracha Hutanuwatr, an activist and former Buddhist monk, organized a conference of fellow Buddhists in Uthai Thani province to discuss the "crisis in big *B* Buddhism" and how they might create a different kind of organization. Sulak and his socially

engaged friends talked about the need for an international network or forum for cooperation, coordination, and support to work head-on with challenges that big *B* Buddhists were unable or unwilling to deal with like rural and urban poverty, the detrimental effects of mass consumerism, the oppression of women, the degradation of the environment, and destructiveness of violence and war.

The gathering convened in February of 1989 on a traditional Thai houseboat owned by Nilchawee's family. There were monks and nuns, meditators and radical activists, professors and bureaucrats—in all, three dozen individuals from eleven countries, mostly though not exclusively Buddhists. Clerics from three Japanese Buddhist sects were represented: Rev. Teruo Maruyama, a Nichiren priest; Rev. Ryowa Suzuki from the Jodo Shinsu Pure Land school; and Rev. Yamada from the Seizan branch of the Jodo Pure Land school. Ven. Rewata Dhamma, a Burmese monk who later founded the Birmingham Buddhist Vihara in England, attended, as did Chatsumarn Kabilsingh, who became the first woman of modern times to be take full ordination as a Buddhist nun in Thailand, assuming the name Dhammananda Bhikkuni. Santikaro, an American monk who was Buddhadasa's primary translator, was in attendance, and David Arnott represented the UK. A number of Sulak's acolytes were present as well.

The result of the three-day conference was the creation of the International Network of Engaged Buddhists (INEB), the organization that has since had the widest worldwide reach of any of Sulak's endeavors.

Previous page, top: Sulak, Maha Ghosananda, and His Holiness the Dalai Lama at the National Cathedral in Washington, DC, in May 1997.

Previous page, bottom: Sulak with A. T. Ariyaratne, Stella and David Chappell.

There was a lively debate about the organizing principles and structure. Sulak's experience as coordinator of the very compartmentalized ACFOD gave him the idea of having almost no regulations for INEB, which would be instead a "loose network of spiritually connected friends with no central authority." Though some members wanted a formal structure, Sulak's view prevailed. A few of the Westerners in the group suggested that to be part of network, individuals must, at a minimum, commit themselves to the five Buddhist precepts (abstention from killing, stealing, lying, sexual misconduct, and intoxicants). The Japanese, wanting the group to focus solely on Asian issues, suggested renaming it the Asian Network of Engaged Buddhists. According to Sulak, one of the participants even said that he was "fed up with all these foreign Buddhists." Sulak objected to such restrictions, predicting that people from different religions and nations would work within INEB in the future.

"I wanted to organize the network the way the Buddha had established the sangha. I think the Buddha would agree with equality, fraternity, and liberty as our guiding principles. And that it would be international, not just for us Asians!"

During lunch on that day, the ordained monks who took part in the meeting were respectfully invited to sit on cushions on a bench, a common custom in Buddhist countries when offering monks their single meal of the day. Monks are given the most respectful seat because of the number of disciplinary vows that they hold. The rest of the group, including the Japanese priests who were laymen, sat below on straw mats on the floor of the houseboat. As coconut curry, rice, and vegetables were served, Rev. Suzuki posed the question, "I don't mean to be impolite, but I feel as though I must be honest: Why is it that, at this meeting where we are talking so much about equality and fraternity across Buddhist and religious traditions, the monks are sitting higher than us?"

The question spurred deep conversation about how tradition, belief, and assumptions can inhibit spiritual development. The most senior Burmese monk sitting on the bench took the lead and sat on the floor with the others. Most Thai would have seen this as very unconventional if not disrespectful to the sangha.

"I felt it was auspicious that this happened at the founding of INEB," Sulak says, even though he is still the first to maintain that monks should be given honored seating. "We immediately put our egalitarian principles into practice in founding the International Network of Engaged Buddhists."

Buddhadasa Bhikkhu, Thich Nhat Hanh, and the Dalai Lama accepted Sulak's invitation to become the patrons of INEB, representing the three Buddhist vehicles, or routes to enlightenment—the Theravada, Mahayana, and Vajrayana. All three have attended some INEB gatherings over the years but their participation has been more by association than participation.

INEB's growth started with individuals and groups in Southeast and East Asia, and spread to encompass other countries. Today INEB has members and organizations in nearly thirty countries. The Bangkok-based INEB secretariat office coordinates activities, with a handful of staff. The organizational structure remains decentralized. The focus of INEB arises from the concerns of the network members, not from Sulak or others who are seen as elders of the organization. As the network is vast and diverse, so too are its projects, actions, and interests. INEB has supported human rights and social justice for the Burmese during the Saffron Revolution, the Tibetans' right of self-determination, for the Chittagong Hill Tribes in Bangladesh, and continued discrimination against the Dalits ("Oppressed"), even though India's caste system has long been outlawed. INEB has advanced peace and reconciliation efforts in Sri Lanka and elsewhere, and worked on various environmental campaigns, such as opposition to dams, mines, and deforestation. INEB has also advanced the equality of women, especially supporting Buddhist nuns, and has created platforms and tools for socially engaged Buddhist youth to engage in civil society, protest, and advocacy.

INEB was just one of many organizations and foundations that Sulak founded from the 1960s onward. He became known at home and in the West for kick-starting numerous and overlapping humanitarian, religious, and environmental groups, organizations, foundations, and projects—all regarded as alternative by the mainstream. His closest colleagues found it difficult to keep track of all of his projects. As one of Sulak's students said, "So many different groups, often with some of us working simultaneously at different ones. We couldn't even remember the acronyms for all the groups—SNF, ACFOD, CGRS, KKF, TICD, SPDI, INEB, SEM, and there must have been others. I'm not sure Sulak could either!"

Sulak not only supported the groups that he himself started, but he also interacted with and promoted many other individuals associated with progressive groups, including Robert Aitken, Joanna Macy, Joan Halifax, Alan Senauke, and others with the Buddhist Peace Fellowship in America; lent logistical supported to Ven. Maha Ghosananda and Rev. Peter L. Pond's peace marches and cooperated with the Inter-religious Mission for Peace in Cambodia; supported reconciliation efforts and worked with A. T. Ariyaratne and Harsha Navaratne of the Sarvodaya Movement in Sri Lanka; set up "Jungle Universities" for Burmese students in refugee camps on the Thai-Burma border; and worked with activists such as Satish Kumar at the Schumacher College in England and the Findhorn Ecovillage in Scotland, to name just a few.

Many times Sulak's efforts to start organizations have fizzled out

Sulak Sivaraksa and the Path of Socially Engaged Buddhism

because of a lack of support, financing, or staffing, or due to political circumstances. Some of the organizations and projects function for a short time and then hibernate until Sulak sees an opportunity to revive and utilize them. A handful of organizations he has founded, like INEB, the Sathirakoses-Nagapradipa Foundation, the Komol Keemthong Foundation, and the Spirit in Education Movement, have endured despite periods of difficulty and been impactful for decades. One important reason for this is that these organizations almost always publish a newsletter or periodical. The written word is essential to Sulak's outreach because it continues to be an effective tool of communication even while Sulak moves on to other work.

Sulak's tendency to overextend himself with obligations to many different people and organizations has inevitably evoked criticism. Wisit Wangwinyu, who was a primary player in many of the organizations that Sulak founded in the 1970s, said, "These organizations always begin with the spark of his ideas. Some work out. Other projects and organizations may be there for a short period and then die. If Sulak were an element, he would be the wind! We are always catching up to his idea. But then sometimes it slows down and is gone. Sulak always keeps remnants of the organizations around, so he keeps them in his pocket—which is sometimes in name only."

Pibhop Dhongchai—who, of all Sulak's disciples, became the closest personally to him—is critical of the way his teacher disperses his energy across many organizations and suggests that Sulak is not skilled at implementing his vision. The Soto Zen priest Alan Senauke concurred when he said, "Sulak starts a lot of things but does not want to be responsible for the nuts and bolts, so he depends on other people."

Some of Sulak's admirers feel that he is emulating the Buddha in establishing a community of like-minded individuals with the same ethos and creed—a sangha—and then turning the organization over to them. Senauke, however, disagrees: "The Buddha didn't form a bunch of organizations. He formed one. And he didn't lose interest in it."

Still, others argue that Sulak's methods have more to do with people than with the organization itself. Viewed in a positive light, Sulak's big vision inspires individuals and generates the momentum for them to manifest his ideas in action. While Sulak serves as the main messenger, his genius lies in eliciting others' voices, opinions, and work to sustain his vision.

David Chappell has called Sulak "a shaman, appearing and disappearing at a moment's notice. Once day he is in the forest in Chiengrai [province], the next at a meeting of social activists in Australia, the next at a gathering of religious leaders in the World Bank in Washington. Even more shamanistic, he uses every opportunity to cure some of the deepest rifts that exist in Thai society, and can produce money to finance the activities of his young Thai acolytes from an empty purse." Anchalee Kurutach, an INEB executive board member, also sees a kind of mystique in the way Sulak operates. "Over the years I have seen Ajahn Sulak make things work by getting all the right people together at the right time. Somehow he has a magic of matching people with projects, and then he helps find funding. When the people take it on, they themselves grow, and learn and progress on the path. It is a skillful means of making change happen within the individual, and maybe organizations benefit too."

....

King Bhumibol Adulyadej, Rama IX.

Sulak being blessed by monks.

Chapter 7

Loyalty Demands Dissent

Sulak is a rarity in Thailand—a Buddhist royalist who believes the people are entitled to criticize their religion and their king. The principal target of Sulak's criticism of religion in Thailand has been directed toward the sangha, the body of ordained Buddhist monks. Laypeople in Thailand traditionally revere the sangha because monastics are supposed to lead a simple, austere, and virtuous life, as exemplified by the Buddha and set forth in a code of discipline. Over the centuries, a sangha administrative structure developed that organized all aspects of monks' lives, from the education curriculum to the annual schedule of rituals to the disciplinary code. Today there is the Supreme Sangha Council, made up of twenty-one high-ranking monks, who have authority over the entire state-sanctioned sangha in Thailand. The king appoints the head of the Supreme Sangha Council.

Sulak began to criticize the sangha as early as the mid-1960s—and has continued ever since—when he reproached the Supreme Sangha

Council, as well as the sangha as a whole. The sharpness of his criticism has increased as the decades have passed without substantial improvements. Sulak pointed out many faults in the sangha's monastic institutions, including widespread financial corruption in the temples and lax discipline in the monasteries. He criticized senior monks who "jockeyed for position to gain royal favor instead of spending their time performing their religious duties."

As Buddhadasa and Payutto had done, Sulak lamented the loss of the public's traditional veneration for the sangha as a result of the monks' failure to live exemplary lives of virtue. Sulak declared this to be a crisis for the sangha, one that struck at the core of the nation's spiritual identity.

Sulak deemed several factors responsible for this crisis, but the root cause lay in numerous misguided sangha reforms that had been instituted a century earlier. The reforms ranged from modernizing the educational system for monks, to a state-sanctioned split in the ecclesiastical denomination into the Dhammayuttika Nikaya branch and the Maha Nikaya branch, to a demystification of the transcendental aspects of the teachings—including removing traditional cosmology and certain meditation practices—because the kings wanted to have their religion backed by Western science. The most pernicious reform, according to Sulak, undermined the traditional moral authority that the monks had over the king. These reforms began under the modernist King Mongkut, Rama IV (r. 1851–1868), but it was during the reigns of King Chulalongkorn, Rama V (r. 1868–1910), and King Vajiravudh, Rama VI (r. 1910–1925), that the sangha became obedient to the crown.

"The monks since the time of the Buddha have represented the wheel of truth and righteousness, the Dhammachakra," Sulak says. "The politicians and king make up the state, and this is where the Anachakra,

Sulak Sivaraksa and the Path of Socially Engaged Buddhism

the wheel of [political] power, rests. There is a necessary dynamic between the two, but truth is always greater than power. If the moral authority of the Dhammachakra [represented by monks] does not legitimize the Anachakra [king], the king must be replaced. This is part of Siamese culture since the introduction of Buddhism. So the Dhammachakra must maintain its distance from the Anachakra, while at the same time advising the king and politicians through the monks' spiritual and ethical standing."

Sulak's deep study of Buddhism in general, and of the Theravada in particular, has positioned him as an authority on the sangha. Still, it was highly unconventional for a layperson to lambast the sangha as Sulak has done. He believes that since the time of King Rama V, who made the monks subservient to the king and politicians, there has been a steady decline in the quality of the sangha, and thus Buddhism, in Thailand. The quality of the sangha, according to Sulak, can be measured by the degree to which they follow the spirit and letter of the disciplinary code set out by the Buddha, and the monks' willingness to speak truth to power.

Sulak's deepest loyalty is to his Buddhist faith—including the sangha—and to the monarchy. He yearns to see them both flourish. But for them to do so, the proper power dynamic between the two must be present. Sulak maintains that only if the sangha is independent from the monarchy can the monks give corrective advice and direct the monarch to steer the right course. The sangha should have this position of critic and adviser to the powerful because the monks are trained in virtue and possess the necessary moral discernment. If the monks are not free to express disapproval, they will fear reprisal from the crown—which is the case today. An independent sangha can give its moral stamp of approval when the king rules justly; but if the monks withhold this stamp of approval, according to Sulak, "the people should chuck the king out."

While Sulak had remained critical of the sangha since the 1960s, he had held back from openly criticizing previous monarchs and their role in usurping the power from the sangha, and for other errors in royal judgment, especially those of King Bhumibol. However, this restraint changed after Sulak learned of King Bhumibol's collusion in the massacre of students in 1976. Sulak believed that his loyalty to the Dhamma and to the monarchy demanded that he express his dissenting views. "I can sincerely say that in this world, there are only two institutions that I believe in so much so that I am prepared to sacrifice my life for them, and those are Buddhism and the Monarchy," Sulak wrote in a 1971 article in the *Bangkok World* newspaper. And because he is so devoted to and cares for his religion and the monarchy, he believes, "My loyalty demands dissent." Nobody is above reproach, in Sulak's eyes, including the king or the most venerated monk.

"This is the point where I have differences with Sulak," former Prime Minister Anand Panyarachun says. Anand was the official biographer of King Bhumibol and very close personally to him. "It is totally presumptuous for Sulak to think that one could influence the King. It isn't done. Sulak thinks he has the right to change the King's character and his personality. Nobody has that right. Nobody."

The majority of Thai share Anand's views on the irreproachability of the king. Thai are taught within the family, at school, and in Buddhist temples that the king is the benevolent protector of the nation who can placate even inanimate forces for the benefit of the people. They learn that the king's intellect, capacity to accomplish his vision, and compassion know no bounds, and so he is worth venerating like a god. His righteousness and royal bloodline grant the king vast vision and capability that allow him, and him alone, to see clearly what the country needs in times of political and moral crisis. This is the belief of a great

Sulak Sivaraksa and the Path of Socially Engaged Buddhism

many Thai, perpetuated by decades of education, social mores, and media influence.

The reverence that Thai have for their monarchy arises from three overlapping cultural narratives. First, there is an animistic belief in spirit protectors of the country, accompanied by a confidence that the king is able to control these forces. Second, there is a notion (which entered Siam via Hinduism between the fifth and twelfth centuries) that a monarch is a living god (*devaraja*), who has sacred blood and is thus semidivine. Third, there is the Buddhist idea of a righteous king (*dhammaraja*), whose legitimacy derives from a storehouse of personal spiritual merit that makes it impossible for the monarch to act in an unvirtuous manner. Today 95 percent of Thai are said to follow Theravada Buddhism, but animism and Hindu beliefs remain strong, especially the faith in the king as a living god.

How did the Thai monarchy, which was stripped of its absolute power in 1932, rise to capture the devotion and obedience of a nation, and regain tremendous political influence?

While the 1932 revolution in Thailand did strip the monarchy of its absolute status, the institution continued as a constitutional monarchy. The Thai royal family resided in the United States and Switzerland in the 1930s and '40s, during which time they had no wish to return and play a significant role. A regent acted on behalf of the king as the monarchy faded from importance for twenty-five years. However, stalwart royalists who would benefit from the return of a robust monarchy were continually searching for ways to reassert the powers of the crown. Their wait was extended when the well-liked King Ananda was found dead in his royal bedchamber in June 1946. His younger brother, Prince Bhumibol, left Bangkok before the hundred-day mourning period concluded to resume his university studies in Switzerland. Bhumibol returned to Thailand to be crowned King Rama IX in May 1950. During Phibun's second dictatorial regime, from 1948 to 1957, the dictator kept Bhumibol out of the public sphere. But after Sarit removed Phibun from power in 1957, Sarit decided to bring the monarchy out of its relative obscurity. He thought it beneficial to project internationally an image of Thailand's "modern king" and allowed King Bhumibol to travel to the UK (where Sulak covered the royal visit for the BBC, as described earlier) and elsewhere in Europe and the United States.

Sarit also began a wholesale revival of the monarchy as a unifying symbol for the nation. During the political upheaval in Thailand and the region as the Vietnam War raged, he seized the opportunity to prop up Bhumibol as a representation of righteousness in the fight against Communism. The US military advisers in Thailand coordinated and helped fund the revival of the monarchy. The palace and royalists had long been waiting for this revival, and it was what Paul Handley, author of *The King Never Smiles*, called the "revenge of the monarchists." Sarit and the royalist media began to create a public image of a studious and modern king, capable of initiating hundreds of "Royal Projects" for the impoverished in rural areas. At a time when the public was fearful of Communists from without and within, the King demonstrated that humanitarian deeds were more important than political fights. The nation watched King Bhumibol nightly on state television, planting rice with villagers, donning a hard hat to inspect newly constructed bridges, and talking with rural children at schools—all part of the many royal development schemes—demonstrating that he was a righteous and compassionate ruler. These hagiographic newscasts and radio reports were effective as a public ritual of admiration, but they were more theater than reality. The King played his role as enlightened engineer with pen and paper and binoculars at the ready, a tireless humanitarian among the

Sulak Sivaraksa and the Path of Socially Engaged Buddhism

rural poor, ever pensive, creative, and deeply empathetic. He was also shown as a contemporary and civilized monarch who enjoyed sailing, composing jazz on the saxophone, and taking photographs with the latest-model cameras.

The strategic burnishing of King Bhumibol's image was accompanied by benevolent narratives of the entire history of the monarchy going back to the thirteenth century. Royal traditions and ideology were invented to establish King Bhumibol as a symbol of the nation in the twentieth century. This reimagining of history and the fabrication of rituals of legitimacy were used as a basis for the royal ideology that depicted King Bhumibol as fatherly, sacrosanct, and—because it was politically fashionable—democratic. It was not long before the populace was convinced that Bhumibol's saintly qualities rivaled those of the Buddha. In nearly every home, business, school, and noodle shop, his photo was displayed as a blessing. Cinema-goers stood reverentially as the anthem to Bhumibol was played before the movie. Newsreels showed the King calmly conducting the business of the nation from his gilded seat while staff approached him by the medieval practice of crawling. Volumes that had been penned by past royalists, including many princes whom Sulak deeply admired, were brought back into circulation. These books told of the greatness of the previous eight kings, and other royals, as deeply religious men and progressive thinkers in fields such as art, literature, and science, especially emphasizing how the kings of the nineteenth and twentieth centuries skillfully synthesized Buddhism and modernity. Past kings were credited for preventing Siam's colonization. Any violent, despotic, or wanton behavior by past kings was scrubbed from history and replaced by fantastical accounts extolling their accomplishments that resulted in centuries of prosperity, security, and happiness for the people. Sulak, along with most of his compatriots, had actually believed these fictions.

Then came the reality check of 6 October 1976. How could a semidivine king, deeply compassionate, with a far-reaching vision, knowing the capacity of the men around him, have been involved with the military generals and right-wing nationalists who perpetrated the bloody massacre of students?

The generals, and the King and his court, knew they had a public relations problem on their hands. The palace and the royalists chose not to try and repair the damage to their image that resulted from incident. The palace acted as if it were only a minor disturbance by a few Communists, and made certain there was never a full public accounting of what happened. Simultaneously, royal propaganda was ramped up to an all-time high, in print and on television, radio, and billboards. And, critically, they began to enforce the lèse-majesté laws more strictly, as a political tool to silence dissent.

Lèse-majesté in Thailand is a crime that lies somewhere between treason and blasphemy. The law came into existence in 1908, but it was only after 1976 that its enforcement became widespread—including against Sulak. David Streckfuss writes in the article "Kings in the Age of Nations: The Paradox of Lèse-majesté as Political Crime in Thailand" (1995) that punishment for the crime has increased in modern history:

> As part of the Print Act in the late 1890s, the sentence for the first Thai law of lèse-majesté was limited to not more than three years in the first imprisonment. Although in the 1908 law, the penalty was increased to up to seven years' imprisonment, after 1932 lèse-majesté as a crime seemed to go into a decline. But with the revision of the criminal code in 1957, in which lèse-majesté became not merely a crime against the reputation of the royals but a national security offense; and with the revitalization of the monarchy under

Sulak Sivaraksa and the Path of Socially Engaged Buddhism

Sarit Thanarat and successive governments dominated by the military, the charge has resurfaced to become the epitome of political and cultural subversion. In 1976, the law was revised to make the punishment not less than three and not more than fifteen years. Sulak Sivaraksa argues that the ever-heightening punishment for lèse-majesté has gone hand-in-hand with the military's ascendancy within Thai politics.

Sulak's repeatedly being charged with lèse-majesté in the 1980s and '90s brought more notoriety to his name than he had won in the 1970s for his intellectual brilliance, his dynamism with students, and his editing of the *Social Science Review*. But why would Sulak ever be charged with lèse-majesté when, as a staunch royalist, he has always argued that the institution of the monarchy must be preserved in Thailand? Again, Sulak's words supply the answer: "My loyalty to the monarchy demands dissent."

In 1982 Sulak gave a speech at Thammasat University in which he was critical of the use of public funds to celebrate the bicentennial of Bangkok and the Chakri dynasty. He argued that the celebrations were merely political grandstanding, and he pointed out that the diploma ceremonies for recent graduates had also become politicized because King Bhumibol was handing out every diploma—"a very good advertisement for the King," as he termed it. This was Sulak's first direct public criticism of King Bhumibol. Sulak's friends thought he might be accused of lèse-majesté. In fact, Kukrit had previously accused Sulak of lèse-majesté in 1969 for an editorial in the *Review* in which Sulak lamented the lack of leadership in Thailand by saying, "The only captain we have is the captain of a sailboat"—a pointed reference to King Bhumibol, whose hobby of sailing a yacht was well known to readers of the popular press. Kukrit's complaint did not sway the authorities to bring charges. But in 1982 Sulak was told that his remarks about grandstanding had strongly displeased King Bhumibol. Sulak responded in the newspaper that it was his duty as a social scientist to analyze the impact on the general public of important events, such as graduation ceremonies, even if they involved the monarchy. No charges were brought against Sulak, but tensions mounted.

Sulak's continued writing about issues involving the monarchy, and specifically King Bhumibol, gained him no favors in relieving the tension. Then Sulak touched on the sensitive topic of who had killed King Ananda back in 1946. The reason Sulak addressed the question was that he had reassessed the role played by Pridi Banomyong, the democrat who headed the 1932 revolution, who was accused of plotting to kill Ananda. Not only did Sulak completely change his negative view of Pridi, but he also decided to make an apology and publicly reconcile with Pridi. Sulak argued that Pridi was not a criminal but rather a national hero, innocent of regicide, who had been defamed by those closest to the King.

What had caused Sulak's reverse in thinking about Pridi in the 1980s?

Like the great majority of Thai, Sulak had believed the rumor that Pridi was involved in killing King Ananda. When the media labeled Pridi a Communist because he went to live in exile in China and France after his reputation was destroyed, Sulak's attitude was "Good riddance!" He wrote many articles attacking Pridi. Sulak was a royalist defending his monarch from opportunistic democrats like Pridi. After more than a decade of Sulak's promoting ultraconservative attacks on Pridi in publications such as the *Social Science Review*, *Witthayasan Parithat* (Knowledge Journal Review), and the magazine *Common People*, the elder statesman responded to Sulak's assaults. In June 1972, Pridi published a Thai-language book, *On the Origins of the People's Party and*

Sulak Sivaraksa and the Path of Socially Engaged Buddhism

Thai Democracy. More than seven pages of the slim volume were spent denouncing Sulak as "despicable debris of the corrupt aristocracy, a social parasite, and an arrogant, selfish scavenger." Sulak seethed with anger upon reading it and published a counter-article in the magazine *Future*, of which he was the editor.

As the public duel continued in writing, Sulak was traveling to attend a conference in England in 1973. There he saw Dr. Puey, who was teaching at Cambridge University. Dr. Puey proposed that he and Sulak go together to speak with Pridi, who was living in Paris. Sulak greatly respected Dr. Puey's views, but he was too proud to meet with Pridi. Dr. Puey suggested that Sulak consider the facts rather than tired arguments and old rumors. Sulak had read *The Devil's Discus* (1964), a book by journalist Rayne Kruger, who concluded that King Ananda had committed suicide, and had heard hushed reports suggesting that the monarch was killed by his brother, Bhumibol. Sulak dismissed these accounts, still believing that Pridi had some involvement. Dr. Puey was not the first elder statesman to reproach Sulak for his overblown rhetoric; former ambassador Direk Jayanama had also done so.

In the early 1980s, Sulak began his own research on King Ananda's death. This inquiry forced Sulak to reexamine completely his assumption about the monarchy as an institution and about King Bhumibol. While Sulak was in this new phase of considering the monarchy, in May of 1980, Poonsuk Banomyong, Pridi's wife, sent Sulak a book, *New Rulings on the Death of King Rama VIII*, which summarizes Pridi's defense of the regicide argument. After reading Pridi's book, Sulak said he felt "like my eyes had finally been opened as to what actually happened." He admitted that he had been "fundamentally incorrect" about Pridi's character and actions.

"The book *New Rulings* acted as a final nudge that freed me from the tightening noose of deceits and bigotry that, for too long, had been asphyxiating my mind and heart; no doubt, a noose that the old cowboy [Kukrit Pramoj] in *Siam Rath* was partly responsible for tightening and pulling," Sulak wrote later.

Sulak wrote to the eighty-one-year-old Pridi, apologizing for his past criticisms and asking for forgiveness. Sulak's confession of errors in judgment was a layman's manner of engaging in *pavarana,* a confessional practice at the conclusion of the monks' annual three-month rainy season retreat. Sulak believes the practice is useful for not only monks but for laypeople as well. And he thinks it is important to confess one's errors or unwholesome actions, not so much in a ceremony or in private to a priest, but openly before others as witnesses.

"Confession of errors is critical to the spiritual path," Sulak says. He later brought *pavarana* practice into some of the groups and organizations he founded.

Sulak finally met Pridi at his Parisian home in early 1982. It was a bold move on Sulak's part, since Pridi was still a political dissident and a criminal in the eyes of the palace and elite circles in Bangkok. But the meeting had for Sulak the significance of a pilgrimage, both of the intellect and of the heart. He noted that after meeting Pridi, he felt the profundity of confessing his faults. This poignant episode in Sulak's life shows that, for all the bravado and intensity that he is known for, to those he deeply respects and admires he will admit his faults openly.

Sulak decided to write about his errors of judgment concerning Pridi, and their reconciliation, in a short book called *Powers That Be.* He wanted his fellow Thai to reassess their own assumptions. Sulak wrote:

> None of my previous subjects were as controversial, brilliant, intelligent, and thoroughly misunderstood as Pridi was. None had

more hordes of enemies than he did. . . . Admittedly, for a significant period of time, I was even his "enemy." Ultimately, unlike any of my earlier subjects, Pridi elicited a fundamental and radical shift in my attitude towards him and the world. Of course, I have always adjusted my perception of individuals and events in the light of new facts. Nevertheless, they were often minor adjustments. On the other hand, concerning Pridi, it seems as if my whole world has finally turned right side up. For too long, like many in Thai society, I have been inclined to uncritically accept some of the grossly unfair tirades against Pridi, and regrettably I did not shy away from using them to denounce or abuse him. My prejudices against him were a turbulent whirlpool that tumbled and destroyed reason and logic; were a tyrannical shroud that clouded my mind-heart. Now, I believe I have achieved a fuller and more balanced view of Pridi and his ideas.

Sulak's change of heart concerning Pridi, coupled with his earlier dismay with the King and ruling elites in the 1970s, completely uprooted his long-held beliefs. As he wrote, "The nightmares of 14 October 1973 and 6 October 1976 highlighted the urgent need for compassion and Dhamma in the country's political governance. Increasingly, I began questioning the virtues and integrity of the ruling circle, where corruption, deception, and abuse of power seemed to have been institutionalized. At least, I concluded that a return to absolute monarchy and aristocracy would not contribute to social betterment and justice."

Sulak wanted the nation to follow his lead in dispensing with the regicide rumors and to recognize Pridi's great accomplishments for Thailand, including the founding of Thammasat University in 1934 and organizing the Free Thai Movement during World War II. It was because of the Free Thai Movement and its opposition to Japan that the United States did not punish Thailand as a belligerent state after the war. Sulak thought of organizing a grand event in Bangkok or erecting a monument in Pridi's name. But Pridi died on 2 May 1983, before he could see Sulak's efforts take shape. After his death, Sulak wrote to the Supreme Patriarch of Thailand asking him to recommend that King Bhumibol, in a spirit of Buddhist reconciliation, send monks to pray over the body of Pridi in Paris and to bring his cremation ashes back to Thailand under royal patronage. Sulak suggested that such an example would promote reconciliation between the different factions of monarchists, democrats, and the royal family. The palace and royalist politicians still feared Pridi as a hero to the students of 1970s, who now held positions as teachers, bureaucrats, and other respected occupations. Sulak argued that Pridi was a true Siamese patriot. He never received a response from King Bhumibol. Despite his sincerity, Sulak's attempts to tell the King what to do were most likely taken as arrogantly misplaced. Still, he felt that his motive was to help the monarch.

"Up to 1970, I was so conservative, and my British education reinforced that. Plato said you need a philosopher king, not democracy; I believed that. I believed this country survived pluralism because of our philosopher king. I had looked toward King Mongkut as a great man, King Chulalongkorn as a great man. But then, in my later studies, I turned around and I see Chulalongkorn was not a great king at all, nor a great man, but rather was very wicked. The more you have the facts, [the more] you change," Sulak said in 2013.

"I never stop trying to learn. I used to take the words of kings and princes as sacred. Now I criticize their words, which makes me more and more Buddhist, in fact, because the Buddha told us not to take anything for granted. We have to examine everything. I try to do this by asking myself whether I do anything out of prejudice or hatred, out of love or delusion. I can't say I'm free of prejudices, but I try to live a life of examination of my actions."

In June of 1983 the Komol Keemthong Foundation published a series Sulak's articles and interviews with the title *Unmasking Thai Society*. Sulak wrote about the misdeeds of past kings and the need for a constitutional monarchy, and warned against the rise of an absolute monarchy. Regarding King Bhumibol, Sulak suggested that he "should be seen as a man with both power and humanity, with both bad deeds and good deeds; not good in every respect." To write anything but praise about the monarch was banned, but Sulak had taken the additional step of suggesting that the King was fallible.

Sulak was traveling in China and Tibet as *Unmasking Thai Society* came off the printing press. After the director-general of the Thailand National Police Department came to know of the book, officers confiscated more than 2,000 copies. Sulak arrived home the day after the books had been seized, and that evening gave a lecture at Thammasat University. During the lecture a student slipped him a note informing him that an arrest warrant had been issued for lèse-majesté charges stemming from statements in the book. Sulak knew that being convicted of the criminal charge, which was nearly always carried out, brought a lengthy jail sentence. He left the campus through a side door and went into hiding with a few confidants to consider his next move.

Fleeing the country seemed to be the safest option. He sent messages to friendly officials in the Royal Navy and Thai airlines who might be able to facilitate his clandestine passage abroad. Flying out of the country was not an option, his contacts told him, so Sulak decided to flee south on a fishing boat in the Gulf of Siam. After three days in hiding while he was waiting for the secret arrangements to be made for passage by boat, the police found and arrested Sulak. He was taken to the Special Branch of the Police, where he was jailed after being denied bail. Although the police treated him with respect, he knew that he had a fight on his hands.

In the crowded jail cell as night fell, a fortune-teller approached Sulak. He reminded Sulak of the men he had seen in the opium dens so many years before, with their vacant eyes and sinewy arms and legs.

"Your nose is like a garuda's; your ears are like the Buddha's; and your eyes are very powerful. You are not an ordinary person," Sulak was informed. He was not one to consult fortune-tellers, but was open to any encouragement as he sat in the dank jail. "I cannot tell you whether you are going to be released today, but you have far to go. This case will make you very famous."

Sulak was released on bail that evening. Sulak and his lawyer began pressing their case with the judge, sent letters to the King expressing loyalty (but not admitting fault), communicated with palace officials, and spoke to the media. International human rights groups took up the case, including Amnesty International, the International Commission of Jurists, and the World Council of Churches. Since Sulak had standing as an academic with the United Nations, the UN secretary-general wrote a letter asking that the case be dismissed.

When it seemed that the lèse-majesté case would be dropped against Sulak, disputes broke out between palace insiders and military officials over having brought the case in the first place; neither wanted to lose face if Sulak prevailed. Sulak was told that the King intervened with a suggestion for the case to be dropped, but there is no written evidence that this occurred. Still, after four months, Sulak and his lawyer were called before the criminal court and told that the charge of lèse-majesté had been withdrawn.

Sulak's acquittal on lèse-majesté charge was a first in Thailand—but it would not be his last.

....

Chapter 8

The Lion's Roar

Two of the most important scriptures in the Pali canon are the Great Discourse on the Lion's Roar (*Maha-sihanada Sutta*) and the Short Discourse on the Lion's Roar (*Cula-sihanada Sutta*). In these discourses, the Buddha likens himself to a lion and equates his teaching, the proclamation of the Dhamma, to a lion's roar.

Rarely did the Buddha ever speak about his own spiritual attainments, as it was not his intention to cultivate reverence toward himself. But these two discourses are unique in that the Buddha does make his greatness known to his assembly of listeners. In the Great Discourse, the Buddha's disclosure of his own supreme qualities comes about because a former disciple has denounced him, trying to dissuade

Previous page, top: Sulak with Pridi Banomyong in Paris in 1982.

Previous page, bottom: Dr. Puey Ungphakorn and Pridi Banomyong in London in 1974.

others from following the Dhamma. In order to inspire confidence in the monks, nuns, and laypeople that he teaches, the Buddha reveals his qualities of self-possessed power and all-encompassing knowledge, which give him the authority to "roar his lion's roar in the assemblies." The Buddha's speech, his message, is a fearless proclamation of Truth that cannot be refuted, like the roar of a lion that silences all the other creatures of the jungle. So powerfully does the Buddha describe the ordeals that he endured on his path to awakening, which led to his attainment of enlightened powers, that one of the monks in the assembly declares that the discourse made his hair stand on end!

In the Shorter Discourse, the Buddha urges his disciples to practice the Dhamma as he taught it, and then go forth confidently and boldly, and "roar their lion's roar" for the benefit of all beings.

So there are two kinds of lion's roar, as described in these suttas: the roar of the Buddha and the roar of his disciples. Sulak's voice of dissent and criticism, and his cries for social change, have been a strong response to the Buddha's call to action.

Sulak's exoneration by the court of lèse-majesté charges for what he wrote in *Unmasking Thai Society* had an invigorating effect on him. His acquittal gave him confidence that he could prevail against future challenges in the courts. He saw it as his duty to confront and challenge the powerful and influential if they were abusing power. And he wanted his students and others to stand up in the face of injustice by the ruling powers. As Roshi Joan Halifax has written, "Sulak is a lion. His great roar awakens the social activist to their real vocation."

Sulak's roar not only continued to inspire his students and social activists, but in 1991, that roar caught the attention of a four-star general, Suchinda Kraprayoon. General Suchinda coordinated a military coup that ousted the democratically elected government in February 1991. King Bhumibol gave his approval for the coup. The general named his military junta the National Peace Keeping Council (NPKC) and appointed the longtime diplomat and royalist Anand Panyarachun as prime minister, though the power remained with the generals and the King.

Sulak was attending the third annual meeting of INEB in Nakhorn Pathom province when General Suchinda carried out his coup. He immediately denounced Suchinda, the NPKC, and Prime Minister Anand as illegitimate. Suchinda did not expect Sulak to criticize him because he had helped Sulak during the 1984 lèse-majesté case. But Sulak did not hold back. During the three months after the coup, he escalated his attacks on Suchinda and the NPKC, calling them "rogues and opportunists."

When a prominent labor leader disappeared a month after he criticized Suchinda and the NPKC, Sulak's friends warned him that he might be next. But Sulak only ratcheted up his denunciations. In August of 1991, the National Student Federation of Thailand and the Coordinating Group for Religion in Society invited Sulak to speak at Thammasat University. Sulak's lecture was titled "The Regression of Democracy in Siam."

"If the student and people's movement are not revitalized, the current National Peace Keeping Council (NPKC) will remain in power for many years," Sulak began his speech to a standing-room-only crowd of 600 students. "Since the first coup of 1947, the military in Siam has not had one new idea. Unfortunately, the civilians are not much better. Deep down they seem to admire those in power, kowtowing like servants to the military. I wish I could name even one person who is respectable and worthy of admiration, but I cannot."

Knowing that his words might be used to charge him with lèse-majesté, Sulak employed his barrister's skills and turned the tables, accusing General Suchinda and all other previous coup leaders—endorsed by the King—of committing lèse-majesté themselves. Sulak reasoned that because the traditional Thai system of justice required all laws to be sanctioned by the king and administered and enforced by the government, any coup contravened this traditional process, and therefore the leaders of every coup were committing lèse-majesté.

Sulak then spoke the words that landed him in trouble:

"Democracy means respecting every person and each other. Everyone is equal and should not have to crawl for diplomas from the King, or pay homage to car tires, like Chulalongkorn University students and graduates. How can human beings manage to live in dignity when they have to pay homage to car tires?"

Sulak was referring to the practice revived in Thailand during King Bhumibol's reign of crawling when approaching the monarch. Some university students actually bowed to the vehicle designated to transport the monarch, even when the King was not inside, in effect paying "homage to car tires."

Sulak concluded with a remark no other Thai was willing to say publicly: "We have to accept the king, the prince, and the princess are ordinary people…. We must somehow help the monarchy exist meaningfully in contemporary Thai society."

Prime Minister Anand said that Sulak "knew in his heart that he did something that he should not have done. He overstepped the boundary."

General Suchinda was incensed by the speech. A warrant for Sulak's arrest was issued for both lèse-majesté against King Bhumibol and for defamation of the general. Sulak received the news from a reporter at the influential newspaper *Matichon*, who reached him and his lawyer by telephone. Sulak told his lawyer that he wanted to fight the case in court. Nilchawee soon arrived at the place where Sulak and his lawyer were hiding out and said firmly, "You are not going to speak anymore." She wanted him to flee the country. Instead, they drove north out of Bangkok to Chiang Mai, where some friends hid him and his lawyer in their home. "I watched on television how they called me a criminal." Sulak recalls in his English memoir that he listened to the head of the Crime Suppression Unit say on army radio, "The old intellectual doesn't realize he is not young anymore. He has a foul mouth. We must knock his teeth in. We must beat him and get blood out of him."

Sulak contacted colleagues in Bangkok and friends abroad to ask for advice. The question was whether Sulak should turn himself in to face the lèse-majesté charge or try to flee the country to fight from abroad. Sulak phoned his German friend Reinhard Schlagintweit, former deputy ambassador to Thailand, who in turn contacted the German ambassador in Bangkok to ask him to help Sulak. The ambassador obliged and offered Sulak refuge inside the German embassy. But how would Sulak make the six-hour journey by road when his face was on television and every policeman and army personnel knew of his arrest warrant?

"The Germans offered to send their diplomatic car all the way to Chiang Mai to fetch me," Sulak says, still surprised and thankful many years later for their assistance. "Because the car had the German flag flying and diplomatic license plates, they did not have to stop at any police checkpoints."

After arriving inside the German embassy in Bangkok, Sulak called home. He knew the authorities tapped his telephone. He told Nilchawee he was safe in the embassy and deciding his next steps. She again told him not to give himself up to the authorities. Other friends concurred because they feared for Sulak's life. The artist Angkarn

Kalayanapong and Pibhop Dhongchai along with some other close acolytes encouraged Sulak to stay and fight. There was a sense among some in Sulak's circle that he ought to take a stand and go to prison like Gandhi. But the Indian writer Arun Senkuttuvan, a top English-language journalist in the region who was following events at the time, says, "Sulak is not a Gandhi. He likes his wine and food and massage. He would have suffered greatly in jail. Sulak is eminently qualified to be a Gandhi in terms of ideas, but not in his lifestyle. This is not a weakness. It is a strength because Sulak is exactly who he is. He knows it and he is public about it."

Sulak did not imagine himself as a Gandhi-like character, but he wanted to fight the charges in court. He telephoned his wife and Pibhop to inform them he was going to give himself up to the police. Sulak said he would walk out the gates of the embassy to meet the police, who had been waiting for him for two weeks. Instead, convinced at the last moment by a lawyer friend who had prepared a getaway car, Sulak fled out a back gate, drove to the border of Laos, and crossed the Mekong River into exile for the second time in his life.

Sulak flew from Laos—using the air ticket of a Laotian student going to study abroad—to Russia, where he bought another ticket, and finally arrived safely in exile in Sweden. He was then able to travel freely in Europe. In July, Sulak wrote Prime Minister Anand to ask for his assistance. "I always say we have to maintain the royal institution, but under the constitution. The king must be an ordinary human being like a *dhammaraja*, a righteous king . . . not a *devaraja*, a divine king. Anyone who wants to maintain the monarchy as a sacred institution above criticism and advice . . . is paving the way for the very demise of the institution."

Sulak was arguing what most contemporary political scientists

Sulak Sivaraksa and the Path of Socially Engaged Buddhism

assert: that absolute monarchy is no longer tenable in modern society. As David Streckfuss, an expert on lèse-majesté in Thailand, wrote in "Kings in the Age of Nations," "The dynamics of the lèse-majesté charge puts into motion a mechanism of suppression that obligates the state to arrest, charge, and try cases, which, in turn, places the state in a dilemma, exposes its vulnerabilities and demands further suppression. The end result is that the dynamics of this law do more damage to the monarchy than its critics could ever hope."

Sulak asked Prime Minister Anand to take his points "into deep and careful consideration, and [have] the results presented to the King." The Prime Minister did raise Sulak's lèse-majesté case to King Bhumibol. Anand said that when he presented the King with the information, Bhumibol grinned and said, "Sulak has not been fair to me."

Back in Bangkok, Sulak's home became a hub and information-gathering point for activists, students, and journalists. Jonathan Watts, a Buddhist scholar from Princeton who began working with Sulak's organizations in Thailand in 1991, recalls that when it became known Sulak had fled into exile, immediately Pibhop, Tepsiri, Pracha, Wisit, Ven. Paisal, and other acolytes coordinated a letter-writing campaign in support of Sulak, addressed to other governments and international bodies like the United Nations. "We knew that he had fled, gone into Laos, at that time. There were a lot of meetings in his house right after he fled. Sulak's family and close circle of students were all there. His wife was always in the center of those meetings."

With Sulak in exile in Europe, Amnesty International adopted him as a prisoner of conscience and invited him to London to give lectures. His case was prominently covered in the Western media, and he traveled to Germany, France, and Ireland, as well as Norway to attend the Nobel Peace Prize ceremony for Aung San Suu Kyi, who was still under

house arrest in Burma. Sulak had predicted in his speech at Thammasat University that the Burmese leader would win the award, even though her chances were considered remote because the Dalai Lama, another Buddhist leader, had been honored with the prize just two years before.

After two months in Europe, Sulak traveled to San Francisco in February 1992. He was received at the airport by Arnold Kotler, the publisher of Parallax Press, who presented Sulak with a copy of his freshly published *Seeds of Peace: A Buddhist Vision for Renewing Society*, a small book of Sulak's writings on socially engaged Buddhism. It became a handbook for many social activists of the 1990s, especially those with a connection to Eastern religions.

In *Seeds of Peace*, by examining a wide range of political, economic, and social problems, Sulak addresses the fundamental question: How can religion contribute to social change? He argues that the sufferings that plague humanity are due to injustices in society, which can only be remedied by social change. And any religious person must take part in this change because it is the mission of every religion to relieve suffering. Religious practice and social change must therefore go hand in hand:

> Radical transformation of society requires personal and spiritual change first or at least simultaneously—[this] has been accepted by Buddhists and many other religious adherents for more than 2500 years. Those who want to change society must understand the inner dimensions of change. It is this sense of personal

Previous page, top: Sulak being greeted by supporters during his trial for lèse-majesté in 1995.

Previous page, bottom: Sulak being interviewed outside the criminal court after his acquittal of lèse-majesté charges.

transformation that religion can provide. Simply performing outer rituals of any rituals of any tradition has little value if it is not accompanied by personal transformation. Religious values are those that give voice to our spiritual depth and humanity. There are many descriptions of the religious experience, but all come back to becoming less and less selfish. . . . Religion is at the heart of social change, and social change is the essence of religion.

Sulak writes broadly about religion in *Seeds of Peace*, and then encourages spiritual aspirants and social activists alike to practice a small *b* buddhism that cultivates mindfulness, tolerance, and an understanding of the interconnectedness of all things. He decries big *B* Buddhism, with its mechanical rituals and ceremonial displays, and its emphasis on titles and patriarchal hierarchies. He warns against institutionalized forms of Buddhism that offer little guidance toward spiritual transformation. Whether it is government-backed clergy or simply large Buddhist organizations, Sulak sees the seeds of chauvinism, prejudice, and nationalism being sown when the Dhamma is used by individuals and groups to advance politically motivated agendas. And to Western Buddhist practitioners, Sulak gives the gentle reminder not to escape into retreats when beyond the meditation hut there is a crying need for social reform.

Sulak reinterprets in *Seeds of Peace* the first five Buddhist precepts of abstaining from killing, stealing, lying, sexual misconduct, and intoxicants. He extends these guidelines beyond an individual's personal practice to society at large. For example, regarding the first precept, Sulak challenges the individual to understand that while we might not be killing outright, we must examine how our own actions might support war, racial violence, or the breeding of animals for human consumption. Re-

Sulak Sivaraksa and the Path of Socially Engaged Buddhism

garding the precept to abstain from stealing, Sulak questions the moral implications of capitalism and of the depletion of natural resources. Ending political structures of male dominance and the exploitation of women is a natural extension of the precept to abstain from sexual misconduct. And the vow to abstain from false speech naturally raises questions about the false and biased views voiced by mass media and mainstream education. Finally, Sulak believes that the fifth precept, to avoid intoxicants, deals with nothing short of international peace and justice, since "the Third World farmers grow heroin, coca, coffee, and tobacco because the economic system makes it impossible for them to support themselves

Sulak leading fifty students and activists to protest and block completion of the Yadana natural gas pipeline through western Thailand's National Forest Reserve in 1998.

growing rice and vegetables." While Sulak is known for his fiery speeches, he strikes a more analytical tone in *Seeds of Peace* when he writes about this reinterpretation of the five ethical precepts. "I do not attempt to answer these questions. I just want to raise them for us to contemplate."

Sulak is not advocating a new understanding of Buddhism but rather an appropriate application of the Buddha's teachings to modern socioeconomic and political dilemmas. It is a mistake, he reminds us, to understand the teachings of the Buddha apart from their social dimension. He stresses the need to establish a strong foundation in a self-cultivated practice of mindfulness and awareness, but he does not want individuals to abide in some kind of meditative bliss for long. Once they have gained an appreciation for the interconnectedness of all beings through meditative insight, it is not enough for spiritual practitioners to eliminate the causes of suffering only in themselves; they must also recognize how they may be participating in societal structures that perpetuate suffering for others. Making individual progress on the spiritual path, in Sulak's vision, cannot be separated from aspiring and working toward a more enlightened society.

Sulak's application of the Buddha's teachings to modern society was influenced by the work of the Norwegian polymath Johan Galtung, the principal founder of the Peace Research Institute Oslo in 1959 and currently Professor of Global Peace at the International Islamic University Malaysia. Sulak credits Galtung for leading him into "serious thinking that Buddhists must take on the system rather than focus on individuals."

Galtung coined the phrase "structural violence" in 1969 to describe the institutionalized ways in which suffering is perpetuated in modern society, and Sulak fused this concept with his analysis of socially

Sulak Sivaraksa and the Path of Socially Engaged Buddhism

engaged Buddhism, first publishing his thoughts in *Global Healing: Essays and Interviews on Structural Violence, Social Development, and Spiritual Transformation* in 1999. Sulak continued to elaborate his views on structural violence in his later books, such as *Conflict, Culture, Change* (2005) and *The Wisdom of Sustainability* (2009). Sulak summarizes structural violence as the "systematic ways a society's resources are distributed unequally and unfairly, preventing people from meeting their basic needs." To explain how these structures are maintained, Sulak brings in the fundamental Buddhist teaching how three "poisons" or mental factors are the root causes of suffering for every individual: ignorance (delusion about the nature of reality), hatred or anger, and greed. These poisons are at the root of structural violence in the modern world.

"If we are serious about getting rid of greed, anger, and ignorance in ourselves," Sulak says, "we must inquire how we actively or passively take part in perpetuating the three poisons in society as 'structural violence.' Once we see the interconnections, we can work simultaneously on our own spiritual development and to dismantle the structural violence in society," Sulak writes in *The Wisdom of Sustainability*.

Sulak explains that personal greed—the insatiable desire for accumulation, an ever-expanding possessiveness—manifests on the societal level as capitalism, consumerism, and the extraction of natural resources in a manner that ignores the limits of the environment. He sees individuals' seeds of hatred manifesting in the world as militarism and all the support structures for war. Sulak's harshest critique is reserved for the peddlers of delusion, which is the primary origin of all our troubles—advertisers and the popular media, which promote useless products and unwholesome ideas that lead people away from a meaningful life of contentment and toward poverty and a sense of separation and alienation.

In *Conflict, Culture, Change,* Sulak condemns economic forces of globalization pushed by the United States and other Western powers, as well as transnational corporations, and institutions such as the World Bank, the International Monetary Fund, and the World Trade Organization. He blames this economic system for much of the violence in the world—not just overt wars, but the violence of injustice that condemns the many to unemployment, poverty, and hunger while the few prosper. Economic injustices "provide a breeding ground for hatred and greed," giving rise to further acts of violence. Sulak's main target is capitalism and the forces behind it:

> The demonic religion of consumerism is based on promoting greed, and in the name of this greed all sorts of violence is committed. The mass media, which are controlled by the transnational corporations (TNC), are part of the problem of structural violence. They distort people's worldviews and preach the religion of consumerism. They work hand in hand with TNCs to promote a lifestyle of consumerism and create a global monoculture. Television effectively brainwashes people and acts as a propaganda machine for TNCs. It deludes people into thinking that the more goods they accumulate the happier they will be, even though such a consumer lifestyle is unattainable by the majority of the world's people and is an ecological impossibility, and to try to attain this unattainable goal inevitably leads to the perpetuation of this structural violence.

Considering how to deconstruct structural violence, Sulak returns, in his speeches and writings, to the need for the individual's practice of mindfulness-awareness, calm abiding meditation, and analytical contemplation. These methods of mind training help dispel the three poisons, allowing the purified nature of one's being to manifest: thus, greed gives way to generosity, hatred to loving-kindness, and ignorance to wisdom. The starting point for this transformation is simply "mindfully breathing in and mindfully breathing out," the basic practice of mindfulness meditation. Sulak recommends mindful breathing to everyone, from college students and activists engaged in street protests, to business executives and UN diplomats. Such elementary advice often leaves individuals impatient for a more concrete plan of action than just attending to the breath. Yet Sulak affirms the Buddhist conviction that the simple practice of mindful breathing leads to a fundamental restructuring of the individual's consciousness. This teaching is a big leap for most worldly people. Sulak cites the Buddha's *Yoniso Sutta* (Discourse on Wise Attention) on how the process unfolds from mindful breathing to ultimately "observing phenomena as they truly are." When the individual gains insight into reality as it is—a web of interconnected relationships that reveals our common humanity and shared suffering—this naturally leads to a shift from the ego-centered attitude to a concern for the well-being of all.

As Sulak's second exile (1991–1992) continued, he traveled in Europe and North America to meet socially engaged Buddhists and to speak about democracy with Thai living abroad. He also stayed for a few months with Alan and Laurie Senauke at the Berkeley Zen Center, where Alan serves as vice-abbot, and a leader in the Buddhist Peace Fellowship. During this time they interviewed him extensively and let Sulak break into long monologues about his life, Siamese history, and denunciations of politicians and political systems. The transcripts form what later became Sulak's memoir in English, *Loyalty Demands Dissent*.

In the spring of 1992, General Suchinda's military junta began to unravel. A *Bangkok Post* editorial stated that although Suchinda had promised "a new political era under which the next election would be free and fair, politicians would be less corrupt and, above all, a fully democratic parliament would emerge," in actuality "this now appears to be a cruel delusion."

Suchinda had promised to step aside after the democratic elections, but instead, pro-military parties engineered the election to win a majority of the seats in parliament and announced that Suchinda would stay on as prime minister. The historian Duncan McCargo wrote in "Populism and Reformism in Contemporary Thailand" (2001), "Here was parliamentary dictatorship in its ultimate form: a parliament whose election had been orchestrated by a dictatorship, which then presented the premiership to a dictator. The greatest shock of all came when Suchinda announced his cabinet. The very same politicians he had decried a year earlier as 'unusually rich' were now sitting around his cabinet table, in a scene strongly reminiscent of the final pages of Orwell's *Animal Farm*" (in which the pigs have become indistinguishable from humans).

Tens of thousands took to the streets of Bangkok to protest Suchinda's government. The general attempted to position himself as the defender of the monarchy, but the pro-democracy protesters were having none of it—they wanted him gone. It was not just students and workers and farmers, as in the 1970s. This time, in May of 1992, Bangkok's middle class, business community, and prominent opposition parties revolted as well. The King watched the chaos unfold but did not contain General Suchinda's authoritarian moves. With the largest street protest in Bangkok since 1973, the army positioned troops and tanks throughout the city, were issued live ammunition, and, as Paul Handley points out, "were told that pro-democracy protesters threatened the country and the holy

Sulak Sivaraksa and the Path of Socially Engaged Buddhism

monarchy itself. . . . There is no sign that the palace institutionally or the king personally questioned this posture, even though the atmosphere on the streets evoked that of the days before the massacres of October 14, 1973, and October 6, 1976."

The numbers of protesters surged to over 200,000, and as they marched late into the night on 17 May, the military stopped them with water cannons when they tried to cross the Phan Fa Bridge. Protesters commandeered one of the fire trucks, then set another two on fire. The army opened fire on the protesters with automatic rifles. Molotov cocktails were hurled as protesters took cover, pulled bleeding bodies off the street, and left others dead on the pavement. Protests continued the next day as the military arrested more than 3,000 demonstrators; the army reportedly killed more than 200. This time the killing of Thai by their own military was named Black May. Sulak was in Canada at the time, and reporters from *The Independent*, the *New York Times*, and the *Boston Globe* called for his thoughts. Sulak reiterated that Black May "was just like the massacre of October 6, 1976."

On 20 May, after the killings, King Bhumibol acted. A carefully stage-crafted scene on national television showed the King reprimanding Suchinda and the leader of the protest, Chamlong Srimuang. Suchinda and Chamlong were kneeling on the ground before the monarch. The scene was "mythologized into a triumph for the monarchy," according to McCargo in "Network Monarchy and the Legitimacy Crisis in Thailand" (2005). This legendary episode in the myth-making of King Bhumibol created the appearance that the benevolent monarch had skillfully interceded to restore democracy for the benefit of his subjects in the kingdom. But the fact is that, as in the 1970s, Bhumibol was not on the side of the people, but instead had been behind the generals who ordered soldiers to fire on them. King Bhumibol repeatedly showed that he preferred that the generals rule rather than civilians. Although the King was given credit for restoring democracy after the bloodshed of Black May, just as he had taken credit for 1973, the facts do not match the royal narrative.

Following King Bhumibol's reprimand of Suchinda, the general stepped down and Anand Panyarachun was named prime minister again. Anand sent a message to Sulak that he could return to Thailand but that the charges of lèse-majesté stood and he would have to go to court.

Sulak returned to Thailand in December 1992, and much of his time for the next three years was spent preparing his defense and in hearings. His last appearance before the criminal court was on 3 April 1995. Hundreds of supporters awaited Sulak's arrival for the trial. Some tied Buddhist blessing cords on his wrists as soon as he stepped out of the car, some presented him with flowers, and others bowed deeply in silence. Sulak wore the traditional villager *lanna*, or wraparound trousers—a statement that he had adopted in the 1970s to protest the Thai adoption of Western-style clothing. There were yellow-robed monks inside and outside the courtroom, a highly unusual sight because monks usually stayed away from political or judicial matters.

Pressure on the Thai court from international human rights groups and foreign governments and diplomats weighed in Sulak's favor. Observers from the International Commission of Jurists were present. Television and print media followed the proceedings closely. The court usually did not allow a closing statement, but Sulak requested he be given the opportunity, and they agreed.

"I know that to attack the dictator [Suchinda] or the people in power is to bring harm to myself, but I regard it as my duty to encourage the people to see the value of the commoner. I feel that ordinary people should be aware of their own dignity, equality and self-confidence—the

Sulak Sivaraksa and the Path of Socially Engaged Buddhism

basic elements of democracy. I have never submitted to any authority and have challenged corrupt authority all my life. Society will fail if people submit to corrupt authority."

Sulak passionately defended himself against the political nature of the charge, offered examples of his longtime loyalty to the King and royal family, argued for the rights of intellectuals, and explained why the prosecution of lèse-majesté charges in general worked to hurt the monarchy rather than preserve it. It was a skillful argument and one that was quoted later by historians and judicial law reporters.

The judges acquitted the accused on all charges. Once again, Sulak had prevailed.

In October 1995, in the wake of Sulak's acquittal, he was awarded the Right Livelihood Award in Sweden, known as the Alternative Nobel Peace Prize, for his "vision, activism, and spiritual commitment in the quest for a development process rooted in democracy, justice, and cultural integrity." He used the $62,500 award to found the Spirit in Education Movement.

Sulak's international reputation won him other important honors as well. The American Friends Service Committee nominated Sulak for the Nobel Peace Prize in 1993 and again in 1994. In 1998, he won the Unrepresented Nations and Peoples Organization's annual Human Rights Award. In 2001, he was given the Millennium Gandhi Award by the International Leprosy Union of India. In 2011, Sulak received the prestigious Niwano Peace Prize from the Tokyo-based Niwano Peace Foundation. Katherine Marshall of the Berkley Center for Religion, Peace and World Affairs at Georgetown University, who was part of the Niwano selection committee, wrote that Sulak's work "to bring about change has embroiled him in many controversial issues and many stints in jail. He approaches advocacy with a combination of knowledge, courage, and

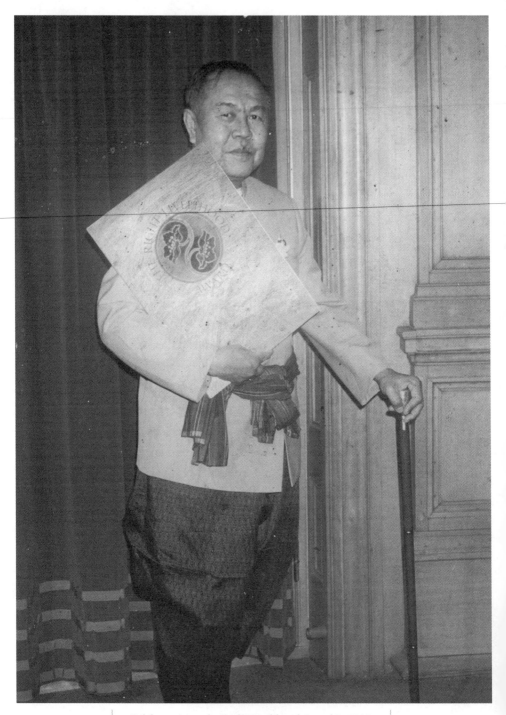

Sulak receiving the Right Livelihood Award in 1995.

absolute commitment to nonviolence. He is widely credited with having mobilized Thai civil society, creating many social welfare and development organizations. All embody two central themes of his work: rejection of development fueled by consumerism, and pursuit of development rooted in indigenous culture and socially engaged religious traditions and beliefs. His organizations reflect an indigenous, sustainable, and spiritual model for change....

Whatever he does, however he does it, at the core of his work is a mission to build a new leadership for change at all levels, within his country and beyond."

....

Sulak greeting Thich Nhat Hahn in 2013 in Thailand.

Chapter 9

Spiritual Friendship

A topic that Sulak weaves into nearly every talk, essay, book, or discussion is spiritual friendship, which he regards as the most important principle in cultivating spiritual development. Because one is often blind to one's own missteps on the path, or because the ego hijacks the loftiest of aspirations, one must rely on a spiritual friend, or *kalyana-mitta*, to point out deviations from the path, provide a reality check, and correct the course. Sulak asserts that spiritual friendship is critical irrespective of one's religious tradition.

The Buddha spoke often about the value of wise mentors and admirable friends to help guide us along the spiritual path. Sulak likes to quote from the *Upaddha Sutta*, in which the Buddha is asked by his close disciple Ananda whether maintaining admirable friends and camaraderie is "half of the holy life." The Buddha responds, "Don't say that, Ananda. Don't say that. Admirable friendship, admirable companionship, admirable camaraderie [*kalyana-mitta*] is actually the whole of the holy life. When a monk has admirable people as friends, companions, and comrades, he can be expected to develop and pursue the noble eightfold path."

Sulak has adopted kalyana-mittata as a very direct and personal approach to effecting not only personal spiritual growth but also lasting social change. The key to spiritual friendship is the giving and receiving of constructive criticism. The kalyana-mitta relationship works in both directions, so that each one receives a critical perspective from the other, and both willingly consider any and all criticisms received. Sulak encourages everyone to seek out virtuous friends, including those outside one's own spiritual tradition, who will provide honest feedback intended to promote each other's personal transformation. Exchanging candid observations with friends is not a comfortable process, but it is one Sulak considers central to his role as an authentic friend. Anchalee Kurutach says, "Sulak is a true friend in the sense that he will never betray you. And for sure he will always be frank with you." And the journalist Arun Senkuttuvan, who was a student when he met Sulak, said of him, "He was a reassuring optimist for us. He could be quite cutting and sarcastic, but never cynical. Sulak was always concerned with people, both individually and humanity as a whole."

What are the benefits that Sulak believes kalyana-mitta offers? For one, a sane, lucid perspective that warns friends when they are being too speedy in body or mind, because such lack of mindfulness can lead to harming oneself or others. There is power in slowing down, and wisdom in becoming (to quote T. S. Eliot) a "still point in the turning world." Sulak often says, paraphrasing Thich Nhat Hanh: "The true miracle is not to walk on water, but to be fully mindful and present of our feet on the ground." Close friends can remind each other to ground themselves and discover contentedness in the present moment, knowing that to cling to the past or fear the future inevitably leads to suffering. Authentic friends will also point out, gently or forcefully, when they see what Buddhism calls the "self-cherishing ego" fueling unwholesome actions on the part of their kalyana-mitta.

Perhaps because of the sharpness of his critical edge, Sulak has not attracted many of what might be called "normal" friends. Yet he comments that maintaining normal relationships "is about ego gratification because friends give you what you want, and when that stops, you don't want to hang around them anymore. But it is more important to have kalyana-mitta, because these individuals will tell us what we don't want to hear." An external voice of conscience rarely soothes the ego, but it encourages us to persist in making diligent efforts toward our spiritual goals.

Sulak has a large circle of colleagues and fellow intellectuals and activists who interact with him in cultural, religious, and political spheres both in Thailand and abroad. Yet these people, with whom Sulak has shared decades of work, rarely touch his emotional being, the part of him that is vulnerable and unguarded. Sulak interacts with them in the spirit of kalyana-mitta. Still, even among his most kindred spirits at international gatherings, Sulak is often a very lonely man. But feelings of loneliness are quickly glossed over by his busy mind, occupied with the need to accomplish the next task.

Sulak takes it upon himself to point out the flaws in those with whom he is close, from his admirers and students to fellow actors on the world political and religious stages. At the same time, Sulak encourages others to shine the light in the dark places where he needs to root out his self-cherishing ego. Over the years, he has tried to become more open to receiving critiques from his kalyana-mitta, but he admits that the walls around his ego are thick, and these walls are undoubtedly guarding Sulak's inner loneliness.

One of the most revealing examples of kalyana-mitta in Sulak's life has manifested in his relationship with Thich Nhat Hanh, or Thay, as he is known, who was a leader in the revitalization of Buddhism in South Vietnam in the 1960s. His highly personal book about the war in his country, *Vietnam: Lotus in a Sea of Fire* (1967), narrates his journey of transforming his religious beliefs into social action and his commitment to nonviolent conflict resolution. It was in this book that he articulated "engaged Buddhism," a notion that greatly influenced Buddhist thinkers in Asia, including Sulak, and inspired spiritually inclined activists in the West. Thomas Merton, after meeting Thay at Gethsemani Abbey in Kentucky in 1966, described him as "my brother" because of their common views.

An accomplished Buddhist scholar, Thay is fluent in Vietnamese, French, English, and Mandarin. He writes in a way that transcends religious dogma and thus attracts readers of all faiths. In his work he places great importance on being "aware of the suffering created by fanaticism and intolerance" and is determined not to be "idolatrous about or bound to any doctrine, theory, or ideology, even Buddhist ones."

"Our own life must be our message," he often says.

Thay went to the United States in 1961 to study at Princeton and soon was appointed a lecturer in Buddhism at Columbia University. In 1963, he returned to Vietnam and continued to organize monks and laypeople in nonviolent peace efforts. He established schools for activists, including the Van Hanh Buddhist University in Saigon; founded the La Boi Publishing House; and wrote essays, books, and poems in several languages, inspiring a generation of peace advocates. As he traveled in the United States and Europe in 1966 with a mission to call for the end to hostilities in Vietnam, he met Dr. Martin Luther King, Jr., who the following year nominated Thay for the Nobel Peace Prize, saying, "Thich

Sulak Sivaraksa and the Path of Socially Engaged Buddhism

Nhat Hanh's ideas for peace, if applied, would build a monument to ecumenism, to world brotherhood, to humanity." While still in America, Thay received messages from Buddhist leaders in Vietnam telling him not to return lest he be imprisoned or assassinated. Thay then began a life in exile that would last thirty-nine years.

Sulak met Thay in Colombo, Sri Lanka, in 1974 at an interfaith dialogue that the World Council of Churches had organized for Hindu, Buddhist, Jewish, Christian, and Muslim social activists. The group took an excursion to pay respects to a famous relic of the Buddha in Kandy, and were received at the temple by Sri Lanka's highest Buddhist dignitary, the Sangha Maha Nayaka. Thay had brought along a statement he had drafted in opposition to the Vietnam War, hoping to collect signatures in support of it. Because of the long history of close relationship between Thai and Sri Lankan Buddhists, Thay asked Sulak to present the statement to the Sangha Maha Nayaka and request his endorsement. But the elderly Sinhalese monk told them, "No, I won't sign this. I don't want to be like the Dalai Lama and lose my country. Monks shouldn't be involved in politics." Despite this disappointment, the occasion caused a mutual respect and camaraderie to arise between Sulak and Thay.

The two men continued their friendship as they both increased their social activism—Sulak in Southeast Asia, and Thay working the halls of power in the West to promote peace in Vietnam. In 1975, Sulak invited Thay to a three-week seminar he was organizing in northern Thailand, supported by the Quakers. Young people from various Southeast Asian countries came together in Chiang Mai to study nonviolence, to explore the power of the written word, to meditate and pray, and to spend time with senior activists like Sulak, Thay, and Swami Agnivesh from India.

While the seeds of Sulak and Thay's relationship had been sown in Sri Lanka, it was on a mountain above Chiang Mai that the friendship blossomed. Sulak watched Thay teach the young activists through his eloquent poetry and his gentle presence. Thay admired Sulak's endless energy and observed how, when the Thai police arrived to shut down the gathering because of "suspicious Communist activity," Sulak reduced the escalating tensions by means of his skillful speech. Thay shared some of his writings—a manual for young meditators—that had been collected into a draft entitled "The Miracle of Being Awake." Sulak experienced the powerful effect Thay's writing had on everyone, including himself, and decided to publish it for the first time in English in Thailand. The title was later changed to *The Miracle of Mindfulness*, which went on to become a worldwide best-seller, translated into more than thirty languages. Sulak and Thay and the Swami gave endless encouragement, each in his own style, to the activists about different ways that a socially engaged spiritual practitioner could change the world.

Buddhism was always concerned with ethical behavior and altruism in social situations, but social activism as a movement was born in reaction to colonialism, foreign invasion, Westernization, and the injustices of oppression in Asia in the late nineteenth century. While today's activists are well known for their political movements, such as the struggles by Tibetan and Burmese Buddhists for self-determination, democracy, and peace, the modern movement of engaged Buddhism has expanded over the past forty years to encompass a vast range of societal issues, including healing the environment, gender equality, community development, help for the dying, and alternative education, to name just a few.

Thay's articulation of Buddhist activism arose in the context of war, while Sulak's evolved in response to globalism, the rise of transnational corporations, military dictatorship, and absolute monarchy. It was Thay who coined the English phrase "engaged Buddhism," which emerged from his writings in Vietnamese that stressed "renewing Buddhism" and "a Buddhism updated" (the translated title of Thay's 1965 book *Dao Phat Hien Dai Hoa*), concepts that he combined with the French phrase *le bouddhisme engagé*. While many academics and activists have since tried to define what engaged Buddhism is, Thay is clear that what the Buddha taught more than 2,500 years ago was an ideal of acting within society, not withdrawing from it. The Buddhist path is by definition engaged with people because it deals with the suffering we encounter in ourselves and in others, right here and right now.

Sulak uses the term "socially engaged Buddhism," a phrase that was spread widely by Parallax Press's publications in the 1980s and '90s and by the Buddhist Peace Fellowship newsletter in America (which today has evolved into *Turning Wheel Media*).

Thay and Sulak continued to work together after the defeat of South Vietnam. Thay still could not return to his country, but from his home in exile in Paris, he worked tirelessly to help his people, and Sulak assisted him in raising money through Bread for the World, the Asian Cultural Forum on Development, and other organizations, to ship rice into Vietnam in the mid-1970s, to help the fleeing boat people, and to facilitate adoptions of Vietnamese orphans.

Sulak found the opportunity to visit Thay in France while he was traveling home to Thailand by way of England in 1976. It was at that time when the bloody coup of 6 October 1976 occurred, preventing Sulak's return, for fear of imprisonment by the military junta.

They first met at Thay's small apartment in Paris and then visited a small farm outside the city that Thay named the Sweet Potato Community. The community later moved to southwestern France and established Plum Village, one of the West's largest Buddhist monasteries, with hundreds of resident monks and nuns, and where thousands of people from all over come annually to study Thay's teachings on mindfulness and meditation. He later established monastic communities in Germany, Hong Kong, Thailand, and the United States, as well as meditation centers around the world, gaining an ever-growing global following.

Sulak recalls his time with Thay in France with great fondness. They would wake in the same room, and Thay would already be seated upright in meditation, well before dawn. Thay was showing by example the disciplined life of meditation. Sulak would rouse himself, and the Zen monk would teach him mindfulness of breathing and other meditation techniques. Although Sulak had learned meditation as a novice monk, he had not cultivated the practice afterward. Such quiet periods, and long sessions of drinking tea with minimal conversation, were uncommon in Sulak's life of constant action. These weeks of meditation with Thay established the foundation for Sulak's future daily practice. Sulak says that he incorporated meditation into his path of socially engaged Buddhism because he experienced for himself its benefits of pausing the body and mind, especially when strong emotions of lust or anger arose. Sulak and Thay also planned future work together and traded contacts of fellow activists around the globe.

Thay and Sulak's meetings became less frequent through the 1980s and '90s. Sulak was busy initiating grassroots organizations and working with activists at home and abroad, including the International Network of Engaged Buddhists, while Thay rose to worldwide prominence as a poet, author, and meditation teacher, with many meditation centers to manage. Sulak kept a wary eye on the rising popularity of his Vietnamese friend. He hoped that the monk who had so skillfully articulated a socially engaged Buddhism that was relevant to the post-Vietnam world would

Sulak Sivaraksa and the Path of Socially Engaged Buddhism

continue to speak out forcefully about situations such as the global arms race, the rise of religious fundamentalism, and violent nationalism. They would sometimes see each other at interreligious gatherings around the world, but Sulak felt that Thay was disappearing behind the layers of his own organization, becoming more interested in increasing the numbers of monks and nuns at his meditation communities in the West. He was concerned that Thay had no real kalyana-mitta to turn to, and that he was "only resorting to monologues to his students instead of dialogues with friends."

"Thay's approach had become too dreamy," Sulak said in 2004. "If you only follow his instruction, then we can forget about socially engaged Buddhism. We all become goody goody. Thay used to be naughty and challenged the powerful. Structural violence is not going to melt away if all we do is concentrate on our breath. It doesn't work like that!"

In 1985, during one of Thay's first teaching tours in the United States, he suggested to Arnold Kotler, a longtime Zen practitioner who had recently become his disciple, that they initiate a publishing house together. Kotler was enthusiastic, and within a year had launched Parallax Press and soon published *Being Peace*, a collection of Thay's teachings that has become a best-selling classic of spiritual literature.

With an immense drive to interact with other socially engaged Buddhists, Kotler met Sulak in 1986. From that meeting, and subsequent correspondence, Parallax Press began publishing Sulak's writings in the United States, including him as a contributor to *The Path of Compassion: Writings on Socially Engaged Buddhism* (1988) and also publishing his *Seeds of Peace* and *Loyalty Demands Dissent*.

Arnold Kotler and his wife, Therese Fitzgerald, were key to Thay's success in America and the West during the 1980s and throughout the 1990s. They were in the Zen master's inner circle. To promote Thay's teachings and social activism, the couple founded the nonprofit Community for Mindful Living (CML) in Berkeley, which later merged with Thay's United Buddhist Church. While there were dozens of individuals in Thay's expanding organization, it was Arnold and Therese who brought him to the masses through the release of more than thirty books, and the ancillary organizations to support Thay's retreats and lectures. With all this exposure to his teachings, Thay's popularity soared in the West, on a par with even so beloved a figure as the Dalai Lama. Thay would soon be teaching Oprah Winfrey to meditate on her television show, and the celebrated actors Ben Kingsley and Benedict Cumberbatch would be narrating biopics of the Vietnamese monk. His acolytes and celebrities saw Thay as nothing short of a modern-day saint.

But in 1999, Thay's relationship with Arnold and Therese came to an unfortunate end. The reasons for the split were complicated, yet all too human. Kotler asserts, in the essay "Letting Go of My Father" in the journal *Inquiring Mind* (Spring 2007), that he was abruptly and without explanation demoted from his position of authority in the Community for Mindful Living and Parallax Press. When Kotler tried to retain some authority, he was fired altogether. Kotler believes that Thay approved the decisions under the influence of another disciple. Rather than push back, Kotler walked away, "overwhelmed by a feeling of personal failure and deep disappointment in the men I'd trusted." He felt great disappointment that the teacher who embodied love, peace, and understanding had treated him so unjustly. Kotler's essay in *Inquiring Mind* challenged the popular saintly image of Thay.

When Sulak heard from Kotler about the situation, he felt he had a kalyana-mitta responsibility to address Thay about the hurt that he had brought upon his student. So when Sulak was in the Bay Area in September 1999, which coincided with a major teaching Thay was giving there, he took the opportunity to call on his old friend. Sulak arrived unannounced at the outdoor venue and walked to where he could see Thay. There was a large entourage outside the tent and a number of "gatekeepers" who prevented Sulak from approaching Thay.

"I was working with Thay before you were born!" Sulak yelled, pointing a finger at the twenty-year-old monks and nuns.

"Ahh, I hear Ajahn Sulak's roar," came Thay's voice. "Please show Ajahn in."

Sulak was escorted to Thay, and after a brief bow of respect, Sulak immediately demanded that Thay explain himself. The interaction was tense, and Thay's attendants were shocked at Sulak's behavior. Nobody in Thay's world ever spoke to him in such a direct manner.

"You better practice what you preach," Sulak said, trying to provoke Thay into a debate. But Thay did not discuss the matter with him. Sulak left the tent and did not stay for the Zen master's teaching on meditation. "I wish I could have helped reconcile Arnie's relationship with Thay, but I failed."

This interaction marked a change in the kalyana-mitta relationship between Sulak and Thay. For the previous two decades, there had been a mutual exchange of ideas, deep listening, respect, and dynamic collaboration. That had now dissolved into a seeming avoidance on Thay's part and bitterness on Sulak's. They did not speak for the next five years.

On two occasions, in 2005 and 2007, the South Vietnamese government cautiously allowed Thay to return to his country to teach and publish books, visit monasteries, and meet with members of his monastic order. His highly publicized visits created controversy among some Vietnamese Buddhist activists who criticized Thay for failing to speak out against the current government's human rights abuses and poor record on religious freedom. Sulak watched, interested, from the sidelines, feeling as though his previous critiques of Thay had been on the mark. Sulak wanted Thay to speak out.

In 2010, Thay came more frequently to Thailand on teaching tours. Sulak had had very little direct communication with him for ten years. Sulak always sent his Buddhist New Year card to Plum Village, and Thay would send greetings to Sulak through his many Thai disciples, but they had not met in person. Sulak wanted to meet with Thay to discuss each other's work and to continue their relationship, which he cherished. "Thay is my teacher. But he is also a friend. We should be able to criticize both teachers and friends with openness and trust."

In 2012 they met in Thailand. Sulak arrived at the five-star hotel where Thay was staying and wasted little time throwing questions at Thay. He asked why Thay traveled with an entourage of dozens of monks and nuns "because of the carbon footprint all the airplane travels create." And why was a fee charged to attend the retreats Thay was holding in Thailand, instead of the traditional Asian practice of offering Dhamma teachings for free? Thay said that there were scholarships available for those who lacked funds, but Sulak would not let go of his point, saying, "Goenka is the model we should follow into the future for Dhamma organizations. No charge for teachings or anything associated with them. People only give what they choose, out of their *dana*, their generosity. The teachings are priceless." Sulak was referring to the model that the Burmese-Indian teacher S. N. Goenka established at his worldwide *vipassana* meditation centers. When Thay and his assistants told Sulak that it was unreasonable not to charge a fee, since they had to rent the venue, Sulak reminded them that the Buddha said that monks and nuns should not deal with money, and that it was the duty of laypeople to provide the needed funds. "Monks and spiritual teachers should not be in the business of making money."

The exchange left Thay in a defensive posture, and Sulak did not feel comfortable afterward. Sulak missed the Thay of the 1970s, a compassionately combative monk who was socially engaged. "Maybe it's because he has become old, or lost his way, or perhaps it is his ego. Whatever it is, it is not the socially engaged Buddhist I once knew."

Still, Sulak wanted to continue to make his point to Thay, in the hope that he would change. So the next year, when Thay returned to Thailand to visit a newly established Thai Plum Village International Practice Center outside Bangkok, Sulak arranged a meeting. The date was Sulak's eightieth birthday. Sulak prepared himself before dawn by writing down bullet points of his arguments, drawing immense energy from his razor-sharp critical mind. He reminisced to his daughter and three other disciples during the drive outside the city about all the different places in the world where he had met with Thay. Meeting Thay was both a joy and a challenge for Sulak.

At the quiet monastic grounds, Vietnamese nuns in brown and gray habits escorted Sulak into a large, open-air, thatched-roof meeting hall. Thay, now a frail eighty-six years old, arrived with the aid of an attendant. Sulak immediately offered greetings like an old friend, but also with the respect of a layman toward a monk, bowing to his feet. He offered Thay stacks of books and printed material about socially engaged Buddhism and contemporary politics. Before Sulak could begin any critical remarks, the Zen master suggested that they drink tea in silence. Perhaps he was trying to disarm his fiery Siamese friend. From a bamboo pole above them hung a clock without numbers—only hour and minute hands that rotated around Thay's calligraphy reading: "The time is Now."

Thay broke the silence by asking Sulak if he remembered when they had met. Sulak suggested that Thay recall his experience for the benefit of the gathered students.

"There were many boring theologians at that meeting in Ceylon in 1974. So I decided to write a poem in Chinese," Thay said, describing how he only used two words, repeated in various combinations, to make a twenty-line poem. Thay wrote on a paper for Sulak to see the two words he used.

The first word was *birth*. And the second word was *death*.

He slowly painted the Chinese characters on a piece of rice paper, repeating the poem in Mandarin. Sulak impatiently waited as Thay moved slowly and with deliberation. When he was finished, he held up the paper and read the poem in English in his soft voice:

> Life after life, the notion of death arises.
> Believing that birth and death exist gives rise to more birth and
>   death.
> When the notion of birth and death dies, then real life is born.
> And real life is to touch continually the nature of no birth and no
>   death.

"So today, Ajahn Sulak, my old friend, we do not celebrate your birth, but rather we celebrate your continuation. Happy Continuation Day.

"How do you feel on your eightieth continuation day?"

"I think your poem is a great gift," Sulak replied. "It reminds me of the impermanent nature of life. And it reminds me to practice more detachment and patience, and to be more humble. Yet I know I want to remain a socially engaged Buddhist. To speak truth to power, and to be more fearless. I hope that my message reaches not only young people but people in power—so that we can come together to deconstruct hierarchal, oppressive systems and replace them with love, compassion, peace, and justice. Maybe this is too ambitious. But with the grace of the Buddhas and Bodhisattas, may it be so. And may I walk in the footsteps of Bodhisattas like you and His Holiness the Dalai Lama and others who follow a noble path."

Thay listened and then said, "It is my understanding that Ajahn Sulak can never die. He cannot die. He will continue in many different forms, in younger and even more beautiful ways. Especially within the younger generation, we can see Ajahn Sulak in them. They will continue Ajahn Sulak beautifully. The most meaningful thing for any activist is to transmit their wisdom and love to the younger generation so that they will continue beautifully. Every moment in life is a moment to transmit what is best in us.

"If you look deeply at the younger generation, you will see you in them, and they will carry you into the future. Whatever love and understanding you have transmitted to them will never be lost. Our movement is continued like this with understanding and love. This will never be lost. The young people will continue with that and make the world more pleasant for the next generation. So I don't need to die in order to be reborn; I have been reborn. You can see me by looking at this body, and by looking at my students. I can see my next life already, as it is now going on. I don't have to die to be reborn, as I am reborn in every moment. That this body is degrading does not do any harm to me."

"This is the best sermon for my eightieth birthday," Sulak said with his hands folded. But the Zen monk was not finished. Thay wanted on this occasion to have the last word.

"This is not theory or philosophy. Every moment is a moment of rebirth. If you look into your body, you see birth and death at each moment. Many cells are being born and dying. So there is no reason to be afraid. Wherever there is death, there is birth. So you cannot take one without the other. If you go a step further, you will see like the Buddha that there is no birth and no death, no being, no nonbeing, only continuation. I don't care about my previous or future life; I care about the present moment because the present moment contains the whole, past and future, and here and there, and this is nirvana. This nirvana is the cooling of all kinds of flames, where there are no notions of birth and death; there is no you and I as different entities.

"I think the structures of violence in the world are in the heart of the people, and if we can first accept politicians' strengths and weaknesses with compassion toward them, then through discussion we can help change their way of feeling and thinking. We have to accept them first as they are, with all their shortcomings, and then peace can come upon mutual understanding. Then the structures can change."

As Sulak arose to depart, Thay offered him an ink painting with a Zen circle (*enso*) around the phrase "You are, therefore I am." Sulak bowed deeply again to Thay. Thay walked slowly to his meditation hut, and Sulak moved quickly with cane in hand back to his van that would take him to Bangkok for an evening meeting with young activists.

This was their last meeting before Thay suffered a severe stroke in November of 2014. After a period of treatment, Thay expressed a wish to go to Thailand. He did so in December 2016, residing at the Thai Plum Village International Practice Center in Pakchong, without receiving visitors but continuing his recovery surrounded by students and friends.

....

The Dalai Lama receives a gift of a wooden cane from Sulak upon their meeting in Dharamsala, India in 1998.

Chapter 10

Skillful Means

When Sulak turned eighty years old in 2013, the Dalai Lama sent him a letter. "I remember our initial meeting during my first visit to Thailand more than forty years ago when we were both younger men. Our paths have crossed many times since then. I continue to admire the work you have done to draw attention to the problems facing humanity and the courage with which you have offered suggestions for solving them. . . . I also appreciate the determination with which you have shown Buddhist teachings and practice to be relevant in the world today."

Sulak had first come to know about the Dalai Lama and the Tibetan struggle many years ago, when he was just a university student. He kept a big file full of Buddhist contacts from all over the world and would call on them during his travels, because he wanted to meet as many different kinds of Buddhists as he could. Sulak often found phone numbers or addresses of Western Buddhists in *The Middle* Way, the journal of the Buddhist Society in England. One such contact was made with an English Buddhist while Sulak was studying French in Switzerland in the mid-1950s. The Englishman invited him for tea in his small apartment in Lausanne, and during their conversation he showed Sulak a small framed photograph of the Dalai Lama and told him that he had immense respect for the Tibetan lama.

"Do you believe in all that reincarnation business?" Sulak skeptically asked. Theravada Buddhism does not emphasize the doctrine of rebirth, nor a system through which reincarnate lamas (tulkus) are identified, as is found in Tibetan Buddhism.

"I can't positively say," the Englishman remarked. "But when you don't know something to be certain, it is best not to pass judgment."

Sulak held that the Theravada—the earliest form of Buddhism—was superior to all other Buddhist denominations. He had been taught that Mahayana Buddhism, chiefly known through the school of Zen and Chan Buddhists in East Asia, was a distortion of the Buddha's original teachings. The Vajrayana Buddhism of Tibet and other Himalayan nations is a branch of the Mahayana. Sulak had been told by his teachers in Thailand that Tibetan Buddhism wasn't Buddhism at all, but rather a mixture of superstition and worshiping of a guru, or lama; they called it Lamaism. Such views persist today among many Theravadins in Southeast Asian countries such as Thailand, Burma, and Sri Lanka, although today the term *Lamaism* is rejected as a misrepresentation.

"*Real* Buddhism was *our* Buddhism—this is what I'd been taught," says Sulak. "It was a very arrogant view."

When Sulak saw the photo of the Dalai Lama in that apartment in Switzerland, he did not have a high opinion of the Tibetan leader. Christmas Humphreys had told Sulak how impressed he was on meeting the Dalai Lama in India during the 1956 celebration of the 2,500th

Sulak Sivaraksa and the Path of Socially Engaged Buddhism

anniversary of the Buddha's birth. Still, Sulak was not convinced by the high esteem in which the Dalai Lama was held.

A few years later, in March 1959, when Sulak was working for the BBC, he reported on the Dalai Lama's escape to India following the crackdown of a Tibetan uprising by Communist China, which had occupied Tibet since 1950. Major news outlets around the world were covering the perilous flight of the young spiritual leader and his small band of aides as they traveled by night on horseback over the mountainous terrain in harsh conditions, finally crossing the border into India, where the Dalai Lama was granted asylum. Sulak took a keen interest in reporting on his fellow Buddhist from a political angle.

Many thousands of Tibetans also went into exile into other countries. In England, the Tibet Society was formed in response to the crisis, to collect funds for the Tibetan refugees, to raise awareness of their country's plight, and to work to preserve Tibet's unique form of Buddhism. Christmas Humphreys was appointed vice-president of the Society. Sulak remembers being asked to sponsor the education of a Tibetan *tulku*, believed to be the rebirth of an advanced adept or teacher. "I had no idea what a *tulku* was, but a very fine lady explained to me how Tibetans recognize reincarnate lamas, and they called these young monks *tulkus* and gave them the title Rinpoche, or Precious One. They often become great teachers."

Sulak pledged some of his BBC earnings to sponsor a young *tulku*'s schooling, and later, in Bangkok, he met the Englishwoman Freda Bedi, who had worked with the Dalai Lama to start the *tulku* school in India specifically to train such boys. Mrs. Bedi later became ordained in the Tibetan tradition.

After Sulak returned to Thailand in 1962 and began reading the ecumenical works of Bhikkhu Buddhadasa in 1964, his condescending attitude toward Buddhist traditions other than Theravada softened. But Sulak owes his deeper understanding about the history of Tibetan Buddhism and Vajrayana practices to his British friend John Blofeld, a prolific writer on Chan and Taoism, who had studied with Tibetan lamas before the Chinese invasion. Blofeld was residing in Bangkok after many years of living and working in China. Sulak was impressed that a Cambridge-educated Westerner had immersed himself in Eastern thought—not unlike the way Sulak had studied Western philosophy. Another trait they shared was the love of good food and fine wines, and Sulak especially enjoyed their weekly dinners, with conversations that lasted late into the night.

In early 1967 it was announced that the Dalai Lama would pay his first visit to Thailand in November of that year. Sulak, Blofeld, and Bhikkhu Khantipalo, an English monk, were active in the Buddhist Society of Thailand and were eager to educate the Thai public, in advance of the Dalai Lama's visit, about Mahayana and Vajrayana Buddhism, and about the struggles of the exiled Dalai Lama and the masses of Tibetan refugees in India. They identified the aspects of Tibetan Buddhism most misunderstood in Thailand and published booklets on these topics in both Thai and English—for example, rebirth, the authenticity of Vajrayana scriptures, how laypeople (and not just monks) could teach the Dhamma, and the similarities in the monastic discipline of both Theravada and Tibetan Buddhism. They also wrote about Tibet's historical independence from China and the political injustices and violence inflicted on Tibetans by the Communist authorities in recent events. At the time, it was possible to publish such political writings in journals under royal patronage such as *Visakha Puja* because China and Thailand were at odds. It would be some years, after China's rise in power in the region in the late 1990s,

Bhikkhu Buddhadasa welcoming the Dalai Lama to his
monastery of Suan Mokkh in 1972.

before the influence of the People's Republic of China in Thailand would allow it to dictate whom Thailand could invite or not.

The Dalai Lama's visit was the most anticipated Buddhist event of the year for the Bangkok elite. Sanya Dharmasakti, the president of the Supreme Court of Thailand, who later became prime minister, led government officials to respectfully receive the Dalai Lama at the airport. King Bhumibol was scheduled to meet the Dalai Lama the next day for only thirty minutes, but he enjoyed the visit so much that Bhumibol asked the Dalai Lama to stay for lunch, and they spent their time discussing Buddhism.

The second day, Sulak was invited to a meeting of the Dalai Lama with Western monks who were ordained in the Theravada tradition. Sulak met the Dalai Lama at the famed Marble Temple (Wat Benchamabophit). He took the opportunity to tell the Dalai Lama about the books and journals published in honor of his visit, and to offer him the Thai translation of the Dalai Lama's autobiography, *My Land and My People*, which Sulak had published some years before the visit. This was the beginning of Sulak's personal connection with the Dalai Lama. His efforts to educate the Thai people about the Tibetan struggle continued throughout his life.

In addition to meeting with the Supreme Patriarch of Thailand and King Bhumibol, the Dalai Lama met with Bhikkhu Buddhadasa. The Department of Religious Affairs issued a directive on behavior protocols for monks, which said that no Thai monastics should prostrate themselves before the Dalai Lama. Despite the strict arrangements and sectarian instructions by the Thai government to the monks, when the Dalai Lama and Bhikkhu Buddhadasa met at Wat Boworniwet, they both prostrated to each other, demonstrating their deep mutual respect that was beyond their own traditions. It was a warm meeting of two extremely open and ecumenical monks. Bhikkhu Buddhadasa invited the Dalai Lama to teach

Sulak Sivaraksa and the Path of Socially Engaged Buddhism

at his monastery at Suan Mokkh. It is extremely rare for Buddhist teachings from a tradition other than Theravada to be taught in Thailand, and was especially so in that era. It took a monk of Bhikkhu Buddhadasa's standing to have the courage to make it happen.

Before the Dalai Lama departed from Thailand, he told his secretaries that he wanted to go out in the morning on alms round. It is common to see orderly queues of gold-robed monks in villages and cities of Thailand, Burma, and other Theravada countries slowly walking barefoot, begging for food. The laity place food offerings into the monks' large begging bowls. The Buddha instituted the practice of begging as a way to teach monks humility. And for the laity, offering sustenance was a means by which positive merits, or good karma, could be accumulated. This continues today to be one of the most important features of the symbiotic relationship between laity and monks in the southern Buddhist countries. In northern Buddhist countries like Tibet, Mongolia, and Japan, the custom of the daily alms round by monks was not established. But the Dalai Lama wished to take part in the tradition of Thailand.

Lodi Gyari, then the eighteen-year-old secretary of the Dalai Lama, who had recently disrobed from the monkhood, arranged for the Tibetan leader to take a short walk to beg for food, accompanied by a few Thai monks. Lodi Gyari made sure to be the first to offer food into the Dalai Lama's begging bowl. The young secretary knew this was a unique occasion, likely the first time in the ancient institution of the Dalai Lamas that a bearer of the title went on alms round.

Sulak was out of the country when the Dalai Lama returned to Thailand in January–February 1972. After a meeting with the King in Bangkok, he traveled south by train for twelve hours to meet Bhikkhu Buddhadasa at Suan Mokkh in Chaiya. Bhikkhu Buddhadasa arranged for the Dalai Lama to teach his community of forty monks in a simple setting, seated on a large stone under the jungle awning. The monks sat on straw mats on the ground while chickens roamed freely around them. A few nuns and laypeople from the village also attended the teaching.

The Dalai Lama was teaching the essence of the *Heart Sutra*, a key Mahayana scripture on emptiness, the absence of an independently existing self. Christopher Titmuss, then a monk and the only Westerner at the gathering, recalls, "We, the monks, were curious. We knew nothing of Tibetan Buddhism; took little or no interest in the concepts of Mahayana and Vajrayana. We certainly did wonder whether Tibetan monks observed any kind of *vinaya* [disciplinary rules] comparable to the Theravada *vinaya*. In his benign and kindly fashion, the Dalai Lama avoided any historical differences and asked us the question 'Who is the Dalai Lama?' We were all ears."

The Dalai Lama posed a series of questions:

"Is the Dalai Lama the robes? No.

"Is the Dalai Lama the voice? No.

"Is the Dalai Lama the face? No.

"Is the Dalai Lama the form? No.

"Is the Dalai Lama the name? No.

"Where is the Dalai Lama? There is no such thing, no such being, as the Dalai Lama."

Titmuss recalls, "At the end of his talk, all of us monks bowed down spontaneously to the Dalai Lama. It was a touching moment. His teachings dispelled any historical differences and went straight to the heart of the Dhamma. Ajahn Buddhadasa, the master on the teaching of the emptiness of 'I and my,' quietly smiled."

The Dalai Lama and Bhikkhu Buddhadasa planned to continue the sharing of their traditions, and to exchange monks between Chaiya and Dharamsala. However, after the Thai government officially recognized the People's Republic of China in 1975, the Dalai Lama was repeatedly denied a visa to Thailand. Since Bhikkhu Buddhadasa did not travel abroad, the two monks never met again. Sulak was at the forefront of lobbying the King and the government numerous times to grant the Dalai Lama a visa. The Chinese government continually warned Thailand that there would be serious consequences if it allowed the Dalai Lama to visit. The Chinese government considered the Dalai Lama "a wolf dressed in monk's robes," whose influence was a threat to their sovereignty. Sulak said in the press that it was disgraceful that a so-called Buddhist country would not allow the most famous Buddhist monk in the world into Thailand.

All the lobbying finally did bear fruit, though. There were skillful diplomatic efforts, and eventually, after Sulak arranged for timely editorials in the main Bangkok newspapers to shame politicians and the King if they did not permit the Tibetan leader to enter the country, the Dalai Lama was allowed into Thailand in 1993 for a meeting with a half dozen Nobel Laureates. The Dalai Lama stayed for less than thirty-six hours to meet with Desmond Tutu, Betty Williams, Mairead Maguire, and others who were attempting, unsuccessfully, to visit Aung San Suu Kyi in Burma. Thai leaders greatly feared reprisals from the Chinese government, but none materialized.

Sulak's mission to educate the Thai citizenry about Tibetan culture continued through his publication of books by the Dalai Lama and other Tibetan teachers such as Chögyam Trungpa. And Sulak continued his own education about Tibetan Buddhist culture by visiting Tibetan communities in India, including Ladakh (known as "Little Tibet"), and in Central Tibet. Throughout the years, he has organized Tibetan cultural events in Bangkok and invited Tibetan representatives. Sulak also taught regularly in the 1990s at Naropa Institute in Boulder,

the first Buddhist university in America. His interest in Vajrayana practice has remained lukewarm, but the political injustice in Tibet sparked him to become the leading advocate in Southeast Asia for the Tibetan cause.

Sulak was invited to Australia for the 1989 World Conference on Religion and Peace (WCRP), the largest coalition of representatives of religions in the world, and part of the United Nations network. Sulak was invited because of his reputation as a Theravada Buddhist scholar. The assembly was made up mostly of top politicians and those regarded by Sulak as "big *B* Buddhists." But Sulak rarely declines an invitation, especially if given a platform for speaking. As his wife, Nilchawee, was fond of saying, "There has never been a microphone that Sulak didn't want to make love to."

The Buddhist section of the WCRP had historically been controlled by the Japanese and Chinese delegations, who did not want to include Tibetan religious leaders, specifically the Dalai Lama. Conservative Christians in America within the WCRP, notably the influential minister Homer Jack, were also in favor of excluding Tibetan voices. Part of the reason for the objection from WCRP representatives was that they did not want to anger the Chinese delegation, who were large donors to WCRP. But Sheikh Abdullah Nu'man, Executive Director of the WCRP based in Australia, wanted to invite the Dalai Lama to the 1989 conference in Melbourne. The Sheikh was opposed by the delegation from Chi-

Previous page, top: Sulak introducing the Special Envoy of His Holiness the Dalai Lama, Lodi Gyari, and his family to the Supreme Patriarch of Thailand, Sangharaja Phra Nyanasamvara, in 1990.

Previous page, bottom: Samdhong Rinpoche, Sulak, and Pracha Hutanuwatr at a meeting of peace activists in 1997.

na and Japan. The Dalai Lama's attendance was out of the question—but, the Sheikh was told, a representative of the Dalai Lama could read a message. Yet, as the date of the event drew closer, even that invitation was withdrawn.

Sulak knew the WCRP had shunned the Dalai Lama from the beginning, but when he heard they would not allow a short message by the Dalai Lama to be read by the representative, he took matters into his own hands. Sulak was scheduled to give a speech on the first day. With all 600 delegates in attendance for the opening keynote addresses, including speeches by the senior WCRP officials who had excluded the Dalai Lama, Sulak decided to read the Tibetan leader's message instead of his own prepared remarks.

"It is an honor and a privilege to read a peace message from His Holiness the Dalai Lama," Sulak began, which brought a preliminary round of applause. Even the President of the Buddhist Association of China, Zhao Puchu, was applauding, as he had not put in his earpiece for translation. By the end of the message from the Dalai Lama that Sulak read, Zhao Puchu, Nikkyo Niwano (Honorary President of the WCRP), Homer Jack, and others stormed off the stage in protest.

Later in the day, the WCRP leadership reprimanded Sulak and the Dalai Lama's representative, Achok Rinpoche. After Sulak was scolded for peddling Tibetan propaganda, an Australian Buddhist approached Sulak to give him a gift, a pendant in the shape of a *vajra*, the Tibetan Buddhist symbol for *upaya*, or skillful means. *Upaya* is a penetrating awareness that enables one to handle each situation with both wisdom and compassion, manifesting whatever response is appropriate to the time and place, and the person one seeks to teach or help. Sulak proudly fastened the pendant as a badge of honor to the fold of his traditional Siamese shirt. Later Sulak connected the pendant to a silver chain attached

Sulak Sivaraksa and the Path of Socially Engaged Buddhism

to his pocket watch. It was as if he were giving himself a time schedule for how often he needs to enact his skillful means, his own *upaya*, to whatever situations life brings.

It was through such personal interactions with the Dalai Lama, his representatives, and others that Sulak became deeply committed to the Tibetan cause. It was important to honor the people first; then support for their political issue followed. Although Sulak had deep respect for the Dalai Lama, the two did not develop a close friendship like the one Sulak had with Thich Nhat Hanh. Sulak found his deepest personal connection among the Tibetans with Lodi Gyari and Samdhong Rinpoche, both of whom have been extremely close to the Dalai Lama for the past forty years. Lodi Gyari served for many years as the Dalai Lama's special envoy in Washington, DC. Samdhong Rinpoche, a strict monk and Gandhian, was previously the prime minister in exile for the Tibetan refugee community. Sulak admires Lodi Gyari and Samdhong Rinpoche greatly for their fighting spirit, their long-term commitment to nonviolence, and perhaps most of all, the spiritual practice they maintained in the midst of an all-consuming political life. It has been an elusive goal for Sulak to find balance between his spiritual practice and his political engagement. For decades he has sought ways for his meditation practice to support his activism, and his activism to influence his meditation practice. The balance has not yet been found, so he admires others whom he perceives as having developed equanimity.

Sulak has never wanted to take up Vajrayana Buddhist practices, which involve elaborate initiations, visualization practices, and daily rituals. Still, he has been influenced deeply by practices found in Tibetan Buddhism. He began expanding his strictly Theravada practice to incorporate Mahayana contemplations and prayers after his exposure to Thich Nhat Hanh's teachings. But after Lodi Gyari presented *mala* prayer beads

Sulak and His Holiness the Dalai Lama in Chicago at the Parliament of the World's Religions in 1983.

blessed by the Dalai Lama to Sulak for his seventieth birthday, he began reciting mantras, especially *Om Mani Padme Hung*, the mantra of Avalokiteshvara, the Buddha of Compassion. Since the early 1990s, Sulak has incorporated mantras into his daily meditation practice, especially when traveling on airplanes. It is a startling image for his fellow Thai to see this elder Siamese Buddhist thumbing prayer beads during a flight.

"We don't recite mantras in the Pali tradition. Of course, when we think of *mahakaruna*, or great compassion, we know in the Theravada tradition that this is equated with the Buddha. But we might find that the Buddha feels very far away. Yet, when we put it in terms of Avalokiteshvara, who manifests in His Holiness the Dalai Lama, for me that is real. Very real. You see? For me, when I talk with the Dalai Lama, he is a simple monk, but when I recite *Om Mani Padme Hung*, His Holiness becomes a manifestation of Avalokiteshvara. I think most of my Thai Buddhist friends would never understand this. But for me it is real. Very real."

Sulak is alert to finding chinks in the armor of monks and the hierarchs within religious institutions, but he has remained ever impressed with the Dalai Lama, especially his humility. Whereas Sulak was eventually disappointed in Thich Nhat Hanh's actions and dwindling political direction, he rarely has a critical word to say about, or to, the Dalai Lama.

One exception occurred after Sulak saw a photograph in which the Dalai Lama was drinking Coca-Cola. He mentioned his disapproval when he met with the Tibetan leader in Dharamsala.

"What is wrong with that?" the Dalai Lama asked.

"Coca-Cola is one part of the problem. These large transnational companies do so much harm. And in India they have poisoned the water," Sulak told him. "Even Coca-Cola is part of structural violence."

"What is structural violence?" the Dalai Lama inquired. "Teach me about that."

Sulak gladly took the opportunity to explain his ideas about ways to create less suffering on a societal level through the dismantling of structural violence. "The Dalai Lama always listens," says Sulak. "I respect him so much because he continually seeks new ways to learn. That is usually not the case with these old monks who just want to give monologues and not to have dialogue. The Dalai Lama is extraordinary like that."

In 2012, as Sulak was about to catch a flight from Asheville, North Carolina, to Washington, DC, he received a call from his daughter, who reported that his younger half-brother, Pravit, had died. Sulak had felt a bond with Pravit ever since they were ordained together as young novice monks. Later they became estranged because Pravit was upset about Sulak's characterization of family members in his Thai memoir. The news of his sibling's death put Sulak into a pensive mood. As he sat in the midst of the busy airport, episodes from his brother's life flashed in his mind—their days in school and at the monastery, attending parties together in Bangkok, accompanying his brother to galas dressed in his fully decorated naval uniform—and, more recently, being ignored by Pravit at family reunions.

"I always thought I would die first," Sulak said. "Maybe I should have tried to resolve our differences."

On the short plane journey, Sulak was thinking of his own death, mentally reiterating instructions about his will and plans for a non-elaborate funeral. Then he took out his prayer beads and began to recite *Om Mani Padme Hung*. The next day, at Lodi Gyari's home near Washington, a Tibetan monk conducted a simple Vajrayana fire ritual for Pravit. Sulak watched as the Tibetans chanted in a language he couldn't understand for his relative whom he hadn't spoken to in decades. They prayed that he would take an auspicious rebirth. Sulak gazed at the large portrait of the Dalai Lama that was displayed centrally on the shrine. Sulak was deeply moved by the ceremony.

The next day, on the plane ride home to Bangkok, Sulak said, "I don't really think too much about my next birth. That really isn't my tradition. But still, maybe it would be nice to be reborn in a Pure Land where Dhamma practice goes very smoothly. Is that being selfish?"

....

Above: King Bhumibol and Queen Sirikit of Thailand in 1961 in England. Sulak (*second from right*) was reporting on the royal visit for the BBC.

Below: General Prayut Chan-o-cha, leader of the 2014 coup, kowtowing to King Bhumibol.

Chapter 11

The King Is Dead,
Long Live the King

After receiving the Niwano Peace Prize in July 2011, Sulak departed Tokyo feeling unwell. By the time he arrived home in the early-morning hours, he was losing consciousness. Nilchawee rushed him to the hospital and he was placed in the emergency care unit. His blood evidenced sepsis.

Sulak had long included the impermanent nature of life in his daily contemplations. Now it was no longer a mere intellectual or philosophical consideration: he was facing the real possibility of his own death. He asked Ming to bring his prayer booklet that contained Buddha's discourse on the "Seven Factors of Enlightenment," which he repeatedly recited and contemplated in his hospital bed. In this discourse, the Buddha teaches about the seven supports that lead to awakening, which are mindfulness, discernment of phenomena, energy, joy, tranquility, concentration, and equanimity. Monks also visited Sulak's bedside to recite the discourse, which is believed to have healing powers in the Theravada tradition. For Sulak, contemplating the seven factors was "a direct preparation for death."

"I was not anxious about death. I thought about the Buddha's teachings and also used my Tibetan *mala* to recite the mantra of compassion. I guess I have become a little Mahayana after all."

Sulak had maintained robust health throughout his life and never had a major surgery. He had relied on traditional Thai, Tibetan, Chinese, and Ayurvedic treatments, usually at the encouragement of his disciples, who wanted to keep him healthy. Sulak did not perform daily physical exercises, but he did take a daily early-morning walk and a late-morning massage. He credits this "lazy man's yoga," as he calls it, for his strong constitution. In 2010, Sulak developed a painful and itchy skin irritation that has plagued him to this day. A number of doctors told him that the eczema-like condition was caused from an excess of alcohol, and thereafter Sulak would abstain from wine for a month or two. But he always looked forward to resuming his social drinking, and it was not uncommon for Sulak to need assistance walking home or up the stairs to his room after a night of drinking with friends. Sulak has never hid the fact that he likes his wine, and eats meat. As Nicholas Bennett wrote in *Socially Engaged Spirituality*, "Sulak is not a saint, nor would he claim to be one…. He likes to dance, eat, drink and be merry, as much as to meditate and fast."

After the first week at the hospital, he had many visitors, including his oldest and closest acolytes—notably, Pibhop and Pracha, who Sulak has said were like sons to him. They may have had serious disagreements with Sulak over the years, as have almost all of his close students. But in the end, Sulak is their Ajahn, a bond that is deep and unbreakable. Many other students and colleagues came to his bedside with solemn faces.

Sulak Sivaraksa and the Path of Socially Engaged Buddhism

One person who did not come to Sulak's bedside was his own son, Chim. Sulak did not expect to see him. After failing his final year at Swarthmore College in the United States in the early 1980s, Chim returned to Thailand to work at the Kled Thai publishing company. Sulak and Chim clashed over management styles. Chim wanted a strict policy regarding reprimands for employees who arrived late to work. Sulak disagreed and said most of the workers were at the mercy of the public bus systems. When Chim wanted to sack a handful of workers who were rumored to have stolen from the company, Sulak asked to see hard evidence. Chim had no proof but threatened that if Sulak did not fire them, he himself would leave the company. Sulak sided with his workers, and Chim left. They have not spoken since 1982.

"This is one of my failures in life. Failing to convince my son to speak to me," Sulak says. Chim is on good terms with his mother and his two sisters, and is a successful sales representative for a transnational construction company in Bangkok. Sulak tried to communicate in different ways since their falling out. He recalls how one day, while he was practicing walking meditation, the thought came that he should ask his son "for forgiveness for whatever I may have done. I've told others to reconcile, so I thought I better follow my own advice that I give to others. I may not have been the best father. But I was not unkind to him." Sulak says.

"To those I have wronged, I always ask for forgiveness, just like with Pridi."

Sulak wrote a letter to Chim for Nilchawee to deliver. "I apologized to him and asked him to meet his old man face to face. But he returned the letter unopened. I've tried other ways. Now there is nothing more I can do. It is sad."

With Sulak's health improving in the hospital, he called a meeting with Nilchawee and his two daughters, Khwan and Ming, and the family lawyer. He had recently prepared his will and wanted to read it to them. The family was not surprised when he told them that all of his property was to be given to the Sathirakoses-Nagapradipa Foundation (SNF) to be used for the public good. This included the land across the Chao Phraya River in Thonburi that his great-aunt had given him (via his mother), which currently housed the INEB, SEM, and SNF offices, as well as their home in the center of Bangkok. The will stipulated that his wife and family could live in the house for the rest of their lives, and thereafter SNF would take ownership. In addition, Sulak's vast library was to be divided between Wat Thongnopphakhun, the temple where he had been a monk, and the Wongsanit Ashram. The only material possessions Sulak was not giving away to the public were the two objects most precious to him—the special Somdet To statue that Phra Bhaddramuni had gifted and a golden ring he inherited from his father.

"I want my son to have both. If he doesn't want anything to do with me, then the objects can go to my daughters."

Sulak told his family that he did not want any ceremony or commemorative literature printed for him, as would be the custom. His death should be announced only after his cremation. For such a prominent intellectual in Thailand, it could be expected that thousands would attend his cremation ceremony, with eulogies offered and books published in his honor.

"I don't want any chanting or sermon by monks. My ashes can be interred with my mother's and father's at Wat Thongnopphakhun, and then my friends should have a party and drink wine. No memorials."

Following the example of Bhikkhu Buddhadasa, Sulak's instructions are to have no pomp or ceremony. He asked his daughters not to have his coffin placed in the cremation pyre but rather recycled and donated for a poor person's funeral. Sulak asked monks from Santi Asoke, a new Buddhist movement that had rebelled against the ecclesiastical hierarchy in Thailand, to conduct a simple cremation ceremony with minimal prayers in the courtyard of Wat Thongnopphakhun. Khwan and Ming agreed to Sulak's exacting wishes about what he wanted done following his death. They had not chosen to follow their father's intellectual or activist example, but understood his motivations of detachment. Like Nilchawee, they supported their father whenever he asked for their assistance, and they both have had active roles in the Kled Thai publishing house.

Sulak's hospitalization spurred his colleagues to think about how their work would go on without the presence of Sulak's large persona giving them inspiration and direction. And Sulak, for his part, began to consider his legacy. Historians have recognized the key role that he played in the intellectual and student movements of the 1970s, inspiring NGOs and grassroots organizations in the 1980s, and his work of socially engaged Buddhism and interfaith cooperation from the 1990s onward. "Whether anything that I started will be successful into the future will be seen if real group leadership emerges. One-man shows are never successful." Sulak has never tried to create a lineage of students who embody what he taught. Rather he wanted them to take what he taught, carefully consider it, and then make it their own. He also wanted them to compassionately criticize and depend on each other in the spirit of kalyana-mitta.

After Sulak recovered from his illness and returned home, his first call was to Harsha Navaratne, a Sinhalese civil rights activist, movie director, and founder of Sewalanka Foundation in Sri Lanka. Harsha is the nephew of A. T. Ariyaratne, founder of the Sarvodaya Movement, with whom Sulak collaborated for decades. Harsha had taken over the Executive Directorship of INEB in 2009. Sulak telephoned him to check on a number of projects.

Harsha appreciates that Sulak has provided a structure for socially engaged Buddhists to move into the twenty-first century with a critical analysis of the many dire problems. He agrees with Sulak that a community, rather than one person alone, must lead societal change. He also sees how the dominance of Sulak's personality may have limited the flourishing of INEB and other organizations that he founded. Harsha credits Sulak with clearly articulating the path of engagement, but he believes, "Ajahn Sulak, when he is gone, will be more powerful than when alive. He has given the real engaged Buddhist message, with correct analysis at many different levels. But to bring out the action, it has to be done by a group of individuals. That group's circle of activity will continue to expand beyond Sulak. The Ajahn Sulak who is no longer with us will be a hundred times stronger than the Sulak who is living."

After Sulak turned eighty in March 2013, his activity slowed some, but he still traveled internationally almost every month to lecture and participate in conferences or academic events. Prof. William Klausner of Chulalongkorn University wrote in the foreword to Sulak's book *A Buddhist Vision for Renewing Society*, "Many regret that Arjan Sulak has felt it prudent and advisable to spend so much time abroad. He often seems to be more honored abroad than at home—witness his recent nominations for the Nobel Peace Prize. His heroic and lonely struggle against the authorities in the sixties and early seventies in Thailand often seems to be forgotten as new anti-establishment critics with their unique brands of charisma emerge. One so quickly forgets the changes in socio-political environment which, at present, unlike earlier decades, more readily allow intellectual flowers to blossom."

Sulak Sivaraksa and the Path of Socially Engaged Buddhism

Sulak has not let up on his critiques of the social inequalities and injustices found in structural violence, the ills of consumerism and capitalism, and the uprooting of traditional beliefs, and his emphasis on the need for personal transformation in conjunction with social activism. His relentless questioning of authority continues unabated. But as the new political movements and politicians ebb and flow in Thailand—including the competing Red and Yellow Shirts, and the tumultuous period when billionaire politician Thaksin Shinawatra was prime minister, Sulak's influence has not had as much impact as he would have liked. Even though many of the political leaders of both the Red and Yellow Shirts were former students of Sulak, they had moved away from his orbit. Sulak remains on the sidelines, trying to insert his voice of reason or criticism, whenever members of the media call.

The esteemed historian Nidhi Eoseewong describes Sulak's significance this way: "Sulak has encouraged people to be suspicious of all authority—be it the monarchy, politicians, religious systems, and even individual monks. This is Sulak's greatest contribution. Sulak's standard has remained: first, is their authority in accordance with the Buddha's teachings; and second, does it aim for the welfare of people?"

Professor Nidhi complains that Sulak has not proposed new ideas for solving the manifold problems of the twenty-first century. "Sulak is like many other intellectuals; they live too long. He is past his useful role for society. It was very good twenty or thirty years ago for him to encourage Thai people to question the authorities. But now [that] the Thai villagers have asked the questions, now they need a formula, clearly and systematically stated, for a new society today."

David Streckfuss counters those who criticize Sulak for reiterating the same message for the last two decades: "When a society does not hear something, you end up saying it again and again. You could make the case that if people had heard Ajahn Sulak in the 1980s, then he would not have to have repeated himself."

"Still, it is impossible for anyone like Sulak to retire," Prof. Nidhi concedes. "Sulak has to write on and speak on. That is his role."

In 2015, Sulak fulfilled one of his dreams: to bring his perspectives on alternative education to university-level learning, when the INEB Institute was established. He had tried before, but his efforts never accomplished what he hoped. This time, working with Lodi Gyari, Harsha, and an international team, Sulak drew on his networks, connections, and charisma to raise the needed funds and attract personnel for the institute of higher learning. Classes began in 2016, and the full master's program is scheduled to launch in 2018 on campuses in Taiwan, Thailand, and India. The INEB Institute reflects the two indivisible forms of inquiry and practice of Sulak's life—engaged social action and personal transformation, both grounded in the tradition of Buddhism. From the outset of the planning, Sulak stressed that he wants the Institute to become a leading model in Asia for higher learning, one that integrates personal and social-structural transformation. Its faculty and students, Sulak says, can "build on the traditions of socially engaged Buddhism to develop, test, and implement new practices, and learning strategies that nourish the moral imagination while cultivating peace and reconciliation, environmental healing, alternative education, sustainable economics, and the capacity for spiritual growth and leadership."

On October 13, 2016, Sulak flew from Thailand to central India to meet activists, intellectuals, teachers, and students at the annual gathering of the International Network of Engaged Buddhists. Sulak has participated in every annual INEB gathering of the last twenty-eight years. The 2016 meeting, held at the Nagaloka retreat center in Nagpur,

India, was honoring the social reformer and Buddhist convert Dr. B. R. Ambedkar (1891–1956) and his pioneering campaign against the Indian caste system and its discrimination toward the Dalits (the lowest caste, often referred to as "Untouchables").

Upon Sulak's arrival at the retreat center, two longtime acolytes, Anchalee Kurutach and Somboon (Moo) Chungprempree, were waiting to meet him with devastating news. King Bhumibol—the ninth monarch of the Chakri dynasty of Thailand and the longest-reigning monarch in the world—had just died in Bangkok at age eighty-eight. In many ways, King Bhumibol's life had been the backdrop to Sulak's own life story.

Shocked mourners were pouring into the streets of Bangkok and other cities, clutching portraits of the King. All across the country, thousands wailed in a mass display of grief never before witnessed in modern times. State television began to run twenty-four-hour hagiographical documentaries and photomontages of the King. Radio stations were ordered to play only somber music. Entertainment was prohibited for a month. An official code of mourning was issued, including the proper color of clothing—black.

The profound sadness that blanketed the country was not surprising. For the vast majority of Thai, Bhumibol was not only their righteous king—*dhammaraja*—but also the very embodiment of a god—*devaraja*—whose sacred blood rendered him divine. King Bhumibol was their forever-father, their protector of the Truth and the Nation, their guiding saint in an uncertain world.

But Sulak's reaction to the King's death was entirely different than that of his fellow citizens.

"Our King is dead!" Anchalee said, moments after Sulak stepped out of the car. Sulak leaned his eighty-four-year-old body on his cane, silent, not so much thinking but breathing in the reality that his King was no more.

Then words came to Sulak.

"If I would not have come, the King would not have gone."

Anchalee and Moo were accustomed to Sulak's often startling utterances. Sulak always likes to provoke others. But this terse remark was something even they could have never imagined him saying. *If I would not have come, the King would not have gone.* Suggesting that his own presence could have somehow extended the life of the monarch was, frankly, audacious. Was it arrogant for Sulak to say? Perhaps. Disrespectful? Most Thai would think so. Maybe he was just playing to his small audience. Whatever his motivation for speaking those words, it was vintage Sulak, as illusive and confounding as the man himself.

Sulak's participation in the INEB gathering was muted. He remained in his room to meditate and pray for the King's auspicious rebirth. The next day, when Sulak joined the 500 activists, he asked that they all stand for a minute of silence in respect for the Buddhist monarch. Many of the younger activists were surprised at Sulak's sadness and reverence for King Bhumibol—they knew him for his criticisms of the King, for the repeated charges of lèse-majesté he had faced, for standing up in protest, not in silence. But here was Sulak, raw and emotional—the "conservative radical," forever devoted to Siamese heritage and ready to defend throne and underdog alike, with his intellectual sword of wisdom. In the words of former Prime Minister Anand, "His heart is royalist. His head is slightly socialist."

The international media immediately wanted a statement from Sulak about the King's demise.

"The King is dead. Long live the King," he said. And in the next breath, he called for the abolishment of Article 112 of the Thai Criminal Code, the lèse-majesté law.

When asked if Crown Prince Vajiralongkorn, about whom Sulak

Sulak Sivaraksa and the Path of Socially Engaged Buddhism

had nothing positive to say, should ascend to the throne, Sulak answered, "But of course. This is the protocol."

And what advice did Sulak have for the new king Vajiralongkorn?

"It's the same advice that everyone needs. He needs kalyana-mitta who will tell him what he doesn't want to hear. He must listen to voices of criticism. The more powerful one becomes, the more transparent they need to be."

Judging by the lack of kalyana-mitta around the late King Bhumibol, Sulak was not hopeful that the new king, Vajiralongkorn, would ever hear any criticism. And this lies at the heart of Sulak's greatest disappointment in life—his failure "to protect the monarchy."

What does this mean in Sulak's mind? It means that the monarchy did not change with the times, that it was closed to the needs of the people, that it did not listen to advice or criticism, and that it became part of the political and military power structure of the country. Sulak believes that a constitutional monarchy, one that is not involved in politics, is crucial to the survival of the country as a unifying and stabilizing force.

"I failed to save the monarchy from corruption, and from being irrelevant to the common man. I tried to warn the King in so many ways for many decades, but he never listened," Sulak says. "But at least I can say I was the first one to challenge the sacredness of the monarchy. I always knew I could be jailed for it. But it was important to pave the way for others to challenge the powers that be—from the monarchy to corrupt monks to duplicitous politicians. For change, for improvement, for development. At least I can say I initiated a movement of free expression in my country."

While Sulak admits to his failure to save the monarchy, former Prime Minister Anand believes Sulak is out of place to believe he could

Sulak at his home in November, 2016.

influence the monarchy at all. "Sulak wants to make our King into a person that he would view as a very best and efficient and correct king. He has his own image of a good king, of a proper king, of a righteous king," Anand says.

"What gives Sulak the right to say that he can save the monarchy? This is where the arrogance aspect of Sulak comes in. A person is not a chattel. You cannot sculpt and remake the product."

As Sulak moves into his mid-eighties, there is little evidence that he wants to retire from offering his advice and critique. Those closest to him say he is more patient than ever before, and that he encourages overworked activists to take more time for meditation and rest. His roar has softened somewhat, and he is less demanding of his acolytes. He continues to publish widely in Thai and English, including a number of historical and cultural monographs following King Bhumibol's death. And after General Prayut Chan-o-cha's dramatic coup in May 2014, Sulak published the collection of essays *Love Letters to Dictators*, in which he denounces and advises the military junta. These essays were first posted to Sulak's Facebook page. Sulak does not use a computer or even have a cell phone, but his young acolytes post his comments and short essays on Facebook after Sulak writes them out in longhand.

Sulak meets regularly with the executive members of INEB, SEM, SNF, and the Komol Keemthong Foundation, and fundraises for each of their activities. He continues to travel regularly abroad to lecture. At his home there is still an ever-revolving hub of students and young activists who arrive, usually late in the morning, to have tea with Sulak in the same courtyard where students have sat since the late 1960s, to listen and be inspired, mentored, and given a role to play by their Ajahn.

International activists, writers, and artists still come and go, staying in the guest rooms, and Sulak plays the perfect host in the evening, offering good Thai food and wine.

Sulak says that as he gets older, he wants to find more time for meditation and contemplation, but he always seems to give priority to action, meetings, and long face-to-face discussions with individuals. Whether among his colleagues or acolytes, or in his quiet time in the morning, he continues to look for those elusive qualities that allow the best of the intellectual, activist, meditator, critic, philosopher, and agitator to emerge. In this regard, Sulak knows what he wants, but not always how to create the manifestation.

"I am from a Buddhist country, and the Buddha, like so many wise men of the past in other cultures, cultivated two important qualities that were the foundation for spiritual illumination—simplicity and humility.

"When we begin to develop simplicity in our life, and humility toward others and the environment, we begin to break free of that oppressive net of the ego. Perhaps more importantly, when we cultivate mindfulness-awareness alongside simplicity and humility, we can liberate ourselves completely from our own anger, greed, and delusion. Through this personal transformation, we begin to see the interconnectedness between each other and the environment around us, and with this insight we will begin to find the wisdom in caring for each other, how not to abuse the earth's resources, and how to find respect for other cultures, traditions, and beliefs."

Can individuals really make a difference in a world fraught with pervasive violence and authoritarianism?

How does an individual dismantle structural violence and bring about a more equitable society?

Why is there so much racism, sexism, and discrimination in the media and how can we get rid of it?

And how to accomplish any of this while striving for a life of simplicity and humility?

Sulak continually returns, as his nexus, to the individual's responsibility to cultivate mindfulness-awareness through meditation.

"If we are serious about getting rid of greed, anger, and ignorance in ourselves, we must inquire how we actively or passively take part in perpetuating the three poisons in society. Once we see the interconnections, we can work simultaneously on our own spiritual development and to dismantle the structural violence in society," Sulak said at the United Nations in 2015.

"How should this be done?" asked the UN under-secretary-general.

"We cannot rely only on intellectual input. We should learn how to breathe properly," Sulak said, offering an unexpected meditation lesson.

"This is how to transform yourself from within. Synchronize your head and your heart holistically. Then you can solve humanitarian problems."

"Profound," the under-secretary-general replied before closing the meeting. "Very profound."

....

Afterword

Harsha Navaratne,
Chair of the International Network of Engaged Buddhists

I left my village in Sri Lanka as a young boy to study with my uncle, Dr. A.T Ariyaratne. He was a progressive teacher who brought education out of the schools and started community development as an initial step for social change. He and the movement that he founded, *Sarvodaya Shramadana*, steered our country away from the Western model of centralized development, and I was one of his first students. We learned by walking every inch of the country and practicing *guru kula*, that is, being with your guru to observe him and practice a daily life of service.

In the early 1990s, after twenty years, I decided to leave my uncle. We had had a falling out because of the massive *Sarvodaya* organization, which I felt was wasteful and bureaucratic. I was still committed to social activism and needed to forge my own path. It was a politically volatile time in Sri Lanka. Many of my like-minded friends, who were dedicated to social change, had been killed by unidentified gunmen. So many of us were being harassed, intimated, and murdered. I had to make a decision to leave the country, or stay and work for its betterment.

I decided to stay in Sri Lanka and start an organization that I called the Sevalanka Foundation. We envisioned grassroots development work to achieve meaningful social change in the country. We were successful, however, within a decade, Sevalanka grew into yet another large organization with many flaws. I had become a part of the very thing that I criticized. So I was questioning where to go, whom to talk to, and I realized I did not have a guru or person to follow. It was not possible to return to my uncle and *Sarvodaya*. And then, I remembered four friends from Thailand who had come and lived with me two decades earlier. I remembered their guru, Ajahn Sulak Sivaraksa. I tracked him down at his home in Bangkok on my next visit to Thailand. I stepped into Ajahn Sulak's community of practitioners, teachers, and followers of true Dhamma, and the world-wide community called the International Network of Engaged Buddhists (INEB). After a few years, when Sulak decided to step down as leader of INEB, I was honored when he and others asked me to become its chairperson.

Here in *Roar: Sulak Sivaraksa and the Path of Socially Engaged Buddhism*, Matteo Pistono describes the political and social movements in Thailand and Asia and weaves in great personalities who have genuinely and without any personal gain or glory contributed to the welfare of others. It is extraordinary to read about the pioneers who challenged the status quo with sheer determination and commitment to Buddhist values—and of course, Ajahn Sulak was one of these trail blazers. As Matteo wrote, "Throughout the Buddhist world, there are practitioners who regard their political work and their spiritual path as one and the same. Indeed, two of the most prominent global Buddhist leaders—His Holiness the fourteenth Dalai Lama and the Vietnamese Zen monk Thich Nhat Hanh—are both known for their lifelong pursuit of social justice and their practice of compassion in action. Another Buddhist leader is Aung San Suu Kyi, who returned to the world political stage after being released from fifteen years of house arrest by the Burmese military junta…. And like the work of these socially engaged Buddhists, Sulak's political activism, community organizing, and advocacy for marginalized people are an expression of his Buddhist practice."

In the recent history of South and Southeast Asia, a number of individuals recaptured their traditional values that had been usurped by colonial, self-centered, imperialistic ideas and governance. The foremost example is Mahatma Gandhi in India with his message of nonviolence and self-reliance and his insistence on the power of truth—*satyagraha*—which challenged the British empire. His was both an independence struggle and a social movement. Gandhi was following other similar movements by the likes of Swami Vivekananda (1863-1902) in India and Anagarika Dharmapala (1864-1933) in Sri Lanka, among others. They talked of religious pluralism, unity, and the importance of understanding one's own culture. Ajahn Sulak is a continuation of the work of leaders like Gandhi.

Ajahn Sulak's story is a story for our time—fighting for social justice with the practice of compassion in action. His promotion of social groups in Thailand—intellectuals, academics, monks, nuns, students, farmers, street vendors, businessmen, and community leaders—has encouraged their moral, ethical and kind-heartedness. He works with an irrepressible spirit, ringing laughter, and with authority. His courage, energy, and capacity to inspire and mobilize people is the true live-wire of the present day global engaged Buddhist movement. In reading *Roar*, we see how Ajahn Sulak skillfully transformed obstacles, avoided becoming a long-time political prisoner, and indeed escaped more than once when his life was at risk. Ajahn Sulak's life is all here in *Roar*—please read this book, and contemplate his noble example!

If we want to honor Ajahn Sulak and his legacy, I feel we must build upon his achievements of socially engaged spirituality in innovative ways. Time is of the essence because there is the pervasive feeling around the world of danger, fear and helplessness. We are experiencing a period of degeneration with oppression, violence, marginalization, and capitalist-imperialist mismanagement. Present day social movements must find synergies with like-minded individuals and groups to promote shared values that will ameliorate both local and global problems. This will require vigilance, patience, and attention.

As socially engaged Buddhists we must cultivate and deepen a culture of openness, inclusiveness, silence when appropriate, and dissent when needed. Our lives should be pro-active with positive energy and our actions should serve as an example of nonviolence. The present day politics of centralization, corruption, nepotism, brutality, and extremism are challenges for all of us around the globe. We live in a world where so many governments do not serve the people but run on cronyism, corruption, and with a lack of transparency. Additionally, we must give voice to the internally displaced people, war-affected communities, and refugees who are grappling with re-building their lives. As socially engaged spiritual practitioners, we need to take responsibility to find ways to address these injustices and crisis. It will be important, as Ajahn Sulak has pointed out, to leave behind the usual way of focusing only on individual issues, or simply protesting—we must look in a more interdependent manner. Engagement means to truly engage, to meet the suffering and crisis and injustices head on, with mindfulness and full of self-confidence. I know that following Ajahn Sulak's example, INEB and other spiritual friends (*kalyana-mitta*) and organizations will take up this challenge.

Ajahn Sulak's impact will grow through the many students, activists, artists, and intellectuals he touched in his life. And in the growth, from generation to generation, it will alleviate suffering, or, to quote Ajahn himself, "From a Buddhist point of view, development must aim at the reduction of craving, avoidance of violence, and the development of spirit, rather than of material things. As every individual progresses, they increasingly help others without waiting for the millennium, or for the ideal socialist society."

Unlike other gurus and leaders of social movements, Ajahn Sulak never promoted himself as a leader of a big organization, even though he founded so many. INEB is a fine example of this decentralized network that grows through various inspirations and ripples. Matteo gives us a glimpse of this noting that Ajahn Sulak's role is difficult to categorize, to describe, or to name as one or the other; yet his influence is significant and profound.

Every time I sit with Ajahn Sulak, and enjoy his oolong tea, I learn. He always listens deeply and provides encouragement. I cherish the time I have spent in conversation these last eight years. As Ajahn Sulak rarely remains still, he has taken me to meet a multitude of writers and artists, to listen to classical music, and to visit cultural events, art exhibitions, food festivals, and historical sites. These days, Ajahn Sulak, Somboon (Moo) Chungprempree (INEB's Executive Secretary), and I travel frequently together around the world to bring our engaged Buddhist message to those interested in listening. Everywhere I go with Ajahn Sulak, I see the currents of his activity in the lives of so many. I truly hope his story—the story of *Roar* will not only inspire the global Buddhist community, but anyone who believes the world needs a more humane and compassionate approach to solving the challenges of the day.

I am honored to offer this afterword to the book. I do so as a fellow traveler on this great pilgrimage of alleviating others' suffering. It is my aspiration that INEB will continue to be a leading light in the world of socially engaged Buddhism. True to the spirit of Ajahn Sulak, we know we cannot rest but that we must forge ahead tirelessly. Traditional Buddhist society has its spirit and energy that we will continue to draw from. INEB will also coordinate and support the increasing number of Buddhists in the West who have a unique opportunity, in particular, to positively affect modernity, social structures, and new technologies that cater to a green economy and sustainable development. INEB welcomes how the two Asian giants, China and India, have re-awakened, not only to economic prosperity but to discover their own heritage of spirituality and environment-friendly value systems. And in the Himalaya region, positive change is also happening. The time is ripe for socially engaged Buddhists and all of our spiritual friends to work together for the benefit of all. *Roar* will be a powerful inspiration to all who read it. Thank you Matteo and everyone who made this important work possible.

Epilogue

There is a danger in writing the life story of an individual as dynamic and irrepressible as Sulak Sivaraksa that the book may be published before further significant events transpire. So it happened with the biography you are reading now of Sulak.

In between the completion of the manuscript of *Roar* and its publication in February 2019, Sulak was once again at risk of being jailed for lèse-majesté, or defamation of the king. There was a very real possibility that Sulak would be found guilty of a criminal charge and be sitting in jail in Bangkok when *Roar* was released.

His latest lèse-majesté case in early 2017—which came about after the completion of *Roar*—stemmed from Sulak's remarks made two years prior at a history symposium at Thammasat University. Sulak had questioned whether the sixteenth-century King Naresuan had led his soldiers to victory in an elephant duel against the Burmese, or if the story was part of royal mythmaking. King Naresuan, who died in 1605, is considered a hero today by the Thai military, an institution regularly at the sharp end of Sulak's critical remarks. Sulak told the historians present, "not to easily believe in anything, otherwise you will fall prey to propaganda."

Between December 2017 and January 2018, Sulak was repeatedly summoned before the military court to defend himself. Western governments, nongovernmental organizations, and international human rights campaigners pressured Thai Prime Minister Prayut Chan-o-cha, the Ministry of Justice, and the military public prosecutor not to proceed with the criminal charges against Sulak. There were no signs they would back down. They wanted to silence Sulak, finally. Almost no Thai spoke out publicly in support of Sulak for fear of their own prosecution.

Sulak did not think the military court would side with him, so he decided to petition the king of Thailand. Unlike with the previous king, Sulak had no personal relationship with King Vajiralongkorn. Still, he wrote a letter asking the monarch to dismiss the defamation charge. Some weeks after he petitioned the king, while he was waiting to be summoned by the military tribunal, Sulak received a phone call that King Vajiralongkorn wanted to meet with him—a highly unexpected turn of events. With the help of his wife and daughter, Sulak quickly dressed in traditional aristocratic wraparound trousers and silk shirt, grabbed his cane, and was driven to the Royal Palace.

When King Vajiralongkorn ascended to the throne following the death of his father, many expected Sulak to be one of his harshest critiques because of the widely reported, less-than-noble behavior as the crown prince. But Sulak, ever the monarchist, withheld public criticism because he felt that Vajiralongkorn should be given a chance to prove himself.

When Sulak was ushered in to the meet King Vajiralongkorn, he asked if he might be able to sit in a chair next to the king as his knees did not allow him to sit in a customary deferential position on the floor. Vajiralongkorn granted the request and seemed genuinely surprised with Sulak could fluently converse in the royal dialect.

King Vajiralongkorn, twenty years Sulak's junior, said he had had three questions: What did Sulak think about the future of the monarchy in Thailand? How could the King strengthen the welfare of the sangha in the country? And how might democracy be truly established in Thailand? Sulak's entire life had prepared him to answer these three questions precisely. Vajiralongkorn listened intently for the next hour and half, asking for points of clarification, while Sulak addressed the first two questions. With their meeting drawing to a close, Sulak asked the king if he could provide an answer to the third topic in writing. Vajiralongkorn agreed and said he would read it with interest. Sulak left the meeting with a sense of optimism—not a sentiment toward which he is prone—for his country, and his king.

There was no mention at the meeting of Sulak's defamation case. But less than a week a later, Sulak received a private message from the Royal Palace that his criminal case would be dismissed. On January 17, 2018, the military tribunal informed Sulak they would not proceed with prosecuting his case. No reason was given, but Sulak knew the king had intervened on his behalf.

Bibliography

A Selection of Sulak Sivaraksa's Writings in English

2014

Love Letters to Dictators. Bangkok: Sathirakoses-Nagapradipa Foundation.
Puey Ungpakorn: An Honest Siamese in a Class of His Own. Bangkok: Sathirakoses-Nagapradipa Foundation. Translated into German.

2009

The Wisdom of Sustainability: Buddhist Economics for the Twenty-first Century. Kihei, HI: Koa Books. Translated into Mandarin, Dutch, Burmese, Spanish, Vietnamese, Japanese, and Singhalese. UK edition (Souvenir Press).
Rediscovering Spiritual Value: Alternative to Consumerism from a Siamese Buddhist Perspective. Bangkok: Sathirakoses-Nagapradipa Foundation.

2005

Conflict, Culture, Change: Engaged Buddhism in a Globalizing World. Somerville, MA: Wisdom Publications. 2nd edition published in 2012 (Suksit Siam).
Socially Engaged Buddhism. Delhi: B. R. Publishing Corporation.
Sixty Years of Achieving Peace in Siam. Bangkok: Sathirakoses-Nagapradipa Foundation and Santi Pracha Dhamma Institute.

2001

As editor. *Santi Pracha Dhamma: Essays in Honor of the late Puey Ungphalkorn.* Bangkok: Sathirakoses-Nagapradipa Foundation and Foundation for Children.
"Welcome Address" in *Social Justice, Democracy, and Alternative Politics: An Asian – European Dialogue.* Papers and reports from an international seminar in honour of Mr. Pridi Banomyong's Centenary. Bangkok: Sathirakoses-Nagapradipa Foundation.

1999

"Buddhism and a Culture of Peace" in *Buddhist Peacework: Creating Cultures of Peace.* Boston: Wisdom Publications.
Global Healing: Essays and Interviews on Structural Violence, Social Development, and Spiritual Transformation. Bangkok: Thai Inter-religious Commission for Development and Sathirakoses-Nagapradipa Foundation.

Powers That Be: Pridi Banomyong through the Rise and Fall of Thai Democracy.
Translated by S. J. Bangkok: Committees on the Project for the National
Celebration on the Occasion of the Centennial Anniversary of Pridi
Banomyong, Senior Statesman (Private Sector). 2nd edition published in
2010 (Suksit Siam) and was translated into Mandarin, Tamil, Tibetan,
French, German, Singhalese, Indonesian, and Hindi.

As editor. *Socially Engaged Buddhism for the New Millennium.* Bangkok: Sathirakoses-
Nagapradipa Foundation and Foundation for Children.

As co-editor (with Pipob Udomittipong and Chris Walker). *Socially Engaged*
Buddhism for the New Millennium: Essays in Honor of the Ven. Phra
Dhammapitaka (Bhikkhu P. A. Payutto) on his Sixtieth Birthday Anniversary.
Bangkok: Sathirakoses-Nagapradipa Foundation and Foundation for
Children.

1998

A Socially Engaged Buddhism. Bangkok: Thai Inter-religious Commission for
Development.

Loyalty Demands Dissent: Autobiography of an Engaged Buddhist. Berkeley: Parallax
Press. 2nd edition published in 2014 (Suksit Siam).

1997

"Interviews with INEB Founders—Integrating Head and Heart: Indigenous
Alternatives to Modernism" in *Entering The Realm of Reality—Towards*
Dhammic Societies. Bangkok: International Network of Engaged Buddhists.

1996

"Buddhism and Human Rights in Siam." Vol. 5 of Occasional Papers. Bangkok:
Spirit in Education Movement.

1995

"Present Trends of Buddhism in Siam and a Positive Future of the Sangha." Vol. 7 of
Occasional Papers. Bangkok: Spirit in Education Movement.

"Thai Buddhist responses to the AIDs' Crisis." Vol. 6 of Occasional Papers. Bangkok:
Spirit in Education Movement.

1994

"Biography and Buddhism in Thailand." (Presented at the University of Hawai'i on
30 April 1993.) *Biography: An Interdisciplinary Quarterly* 17, no. 1 (Winter):

Sulak Sivaraksa and the Path of Socially Engaged Buddhism

2–19. Honolulu: University of Hawai'i Press.

As editor. *The Quest for a Just Society: The Legacy and Challenge of Buddhadasa Bhikkhu*. Bangkok: Thai Inter-Religious Commission for Development and Santi Pracha Dhamma Institute.

1993

"Alternative Development from a Buddhist Perspective." Volume 1 of Occasional Papers. Bangkok: Spirit in Education Movement.

Buddhist Perception for Desirable Societies in the Future: Papers Prepared for the United Nations University. Bangkok: Thai Inter-religious Commission for Development and Sathirakoses-Nagapradipa Foundation.

"How Societies Can Practice the Precepts." In Thich Nhat Hanh et al., *For a Future to Be Possible: Commentaries on the Five Wonderful Precepts*. Berkeley: Parallax Press.

"Thai Spirituality and Modernization." *In Buddhist Spirituality: Indian, Southeast Asian, Tibetan, Early Chinese*, edited by Takeuchi Yoshinori. New York: Crossroad Publishing Company.

When Loyalty Demands Dissent: Sulak Sivaraksa and the Charge of Lèse-Majesté in Siam, 1991–1993. Bangkok: Santi Pracha Dhamma Institute.

1992

"Buddhism and Contemporary International Trends." In *Inner Peace, World Peace: Essays on Buddhism and Nonviolence*, edited by Kenneth Kraft. Albany: State University of New York Press.

"Making Buddhism Radical: An Interview with Sulak Sivaraksa," by Donald Rothberg. *Turning Wheel: Journal of the Buddhist Peace Fellowship*. Berkeley: Buddhist Peace Fellowship.

Seeds of Peace: A Buddhist Vision for Renewing Society. Edited by Tom Ginsburg. Berkeley: Parallax Press. Translated into Dutch, German, Singhalese, Italian, and Indonesian.

1990

"A Buddhist Perception of a Desirable Society." In *Ethics of Environment and Development: Global Challenge, International Response*, edited by J. Ronald Engel and Joan Gibb Engel. Tucson: University of Arizona Press.

"True Development." In *Dharma Gaia: A Harvest of Essays in Buddhism and Ecology*, edited by Allan Hunt Badiner. Berkeley: Parallax Press.

1989

"Building Trust Through Economic and Social Development and Ecological Balance: A Buddhist Perspective." In *Radical Conservatism: Buddhism in the Contemporary World. Articles in Honour of Bhikkhu Buddhadasa's Eighty-fourth Birthday Anniversary.* Edited by Sulak Sivaraksa. Bangkok: Thai Inter-religious Commission for Development and the International Network of Engaged Buddhists.

"The Crisis of Siamese Identity." In Vol. 17 of Occasional Papers. Bangkok: Thai Inter-religious Commission for Development.

As editor. *Liberation, Religion and Culture: Asian-Pacific Perspectives. Proceedings of an ACFOD Seminar.* Bangkok: Asian Cultural Forum on Development.

"The Religious and Cultural Data Center for Education and Development." Occasional paper. Bangkok: Santi Pracha Dhamma Institute.

1988

"Buddhism for Society." Bangkok: Thai Inter-religious Commission for Development.

"Buddhism in a World of Change: Politics Must Be Related to Religion." In *The Path of Compassion: Writings on Socially Engaged Buddhism*, edited by Kenneth Kraft. Berkeley: Parallax Press.

"Buddhist Understanding of Justice and Peace: Challenges and Responses to Asian Realities." Vol. 12 of Occasional Papers. Bangkok: Santi Pracha Dhamma Institute.

"Development for Peace." Occasional paper. Bangkok: Santi Pracha Dhamma Institute, Pacific Youth Forum, and Asian Cultural Forum on Development.

"The Religion of Consumerism." Vol. 12 of Occasional Papers. Bangkok: Santi Pracha Dhamma Institute.

"Siamese Literature and Social Liberation." Vol. 6 of Occasional Papers. Bangkok: Santi Pracha Dhamma Institute.

"Understanding a State and Its Minorities from a Religious and Cultural Perspective: The Case of Siam and Burma." Vol. 9 of Occasional Papers. Bangkok: Santi Pracha Dhamma Institute and Thai Inter-religious Commission for Development.

1987

"Buddhism and the Socio-political Setting for the Future Benefit of Mankind." Vol. 3 of Occasional Papers. Bangkok: Pridi Banomyong Institute.

Religion and Development. Translated by Francis Seely and edited by Grant A. Olson.

Bangkok: Thai Inter-religious Commission for Development. 4th edition published in 2009 (Sathirakoses-Nagapradipa Foundation) and translated into Dutch, Burmese, and Singhalese.

"Science, Technology, and Spiritual Values: A South-East Asian Approach to Modernization." Vol. 4 of Occasional Papers. Bangkok: Thai Inter-religious Commission for Development.

"Thai Spirituality." *Journal of the Siam Society.* 75: 75–90.

"Thai Thoughts on the One Hundredth Anniversary of Diplomatic Relations between Japan and Siam." Vol. 5 of Occasional Papers. Bangkok: Santi Pracha Dhamma Institute.

"The Value of Human Life in Buddhist Thought." Vol. 1 of Occasional Papers. Bangkok: Pridi Banomyong Institute.

1985

"Rural Poverty and Development in Thailand, Indonesia, and the Philippines." *The Ecologist* 15 (5–6): 266–68.

Siamese Resurgence: A Thai Buddhist Voice on Asia and a World of Change. Bangkok: Asian Cultural Forum on Development.

1984

"Buddhism and Society: Beyond the Present Horizon." In *Buddhism and Society in Thailand*, edited by B. J. Terwiel. Gaya, India: Centre for South East Asian Studies.

"Culture and Development in Asia." In *Searching for Asian Paradigms: Contribution of Youth to the Promotion of Social Goals and Cultural Values in the Development Process*, edited by C. I. Itty. (Papers presented to Expert Group Meeting on the Contribution of Youth to the Promotion of the Social Goals and Cultural Values in the Development Process, held at Chiengmai, Thailand, 26 October–2 November 1981.) Bangkok: Asian Cultural Forum on Development.

1982

"Review of *Phutthatham (Buddhadhamma)* by the Venerable Phra Rajavaramuni (Payutto)." *Journal of the Siam Society.* 70 (1–2): 164–70.

1981

A Buddhist Vision for Renewing Society: Collected Articles by a Concerned Thai

Intellectual. Bangkok: Thai Watana Panich Company.

1980

Siam in Crisis. Bangkok: Komol Keemthong Foundation.

1979

The Life and Work of Prince Damrong Rajanubhab (1862-1943) as a Historical Testimony of Endogenous Thai Intellectual Creativity. Tokyo: United Nations University.

1976

"After Vietnam, Thailand." *Solidarity* 10 (5–6). Manila: Solidaridad Publishing House.
"Religion and Development." In *Seeds of Peace*. Asahala Puja II. Bangkok: Thai Wathana T. Suwan Foundation.

1975

"Thailand: The Move Away from Military Dictatorship." *Solidarity* 9 (8). Manila: Solidaridad Publishing House.

1974

"Thai Buddhism and National Development." In *Religion and Development in Asian Societies: Papers Presented at the Seminar on "Religion and Development in Asian Societies*," by Heinz Bechert et al. Colombo: Marga Publications.

1973

As co-editor (with Charles F. Keyes and William J. Klausner). "Phya Anuman Rajadhon: A Reminiscence." Bangkok: Sathirakoses-Nagapradipa Foundation.
"The Role of the Intellectuals." In *Trends in Thailand: Proceedings with Background and Commentary Papers*. Singapore University Press.
Siam Through a Looking Glass: A Critique. Collected Writings of Sulak Sivaraksa. Bangkok: Suksit Siam.

1972

Ethics from the Sphere of Knowledge. Bangkok: Social Science Association of Thailand.

1970

"Phya Anuman: A Common Man or a Genius." In *In Memoriam Phya Anuman Rajadhon*. Bangkok: The Siam Society.
"Siam Versus the West." *Solidarity* 5 (4). Manila: Solidaridad Publishing House.

Sulak Sivaraksa and the Path of Socially Engaged Buddhism

1962

As translator. *A History of Buddhist Monuments in Siam*, by Prince Damrong
Rajanubhab. Bangkok: The Siam Society.

1957

"Buddhasana" in *Samaggi Sara*, the annual journal of Samaggi Samagom, the Thai
Association in the United Kingdom. London.

1956

"Christianity in Siam." *Gateway*. Cardiff: Saint David's College.

1955

"Why the Siamese Chose English." *Gateway*. Cardiff: Saint David's College.

Index

Page numbers in italics indicate photos.

N

Naresuan, King, 243

Narong Kittikachorn, 91, 109

Naropa Institute, 211

The Nation, 2

National Administrative Reform Council (NARC), 112

National Labor Council of Thailand, 109

National Peace Keeping Council (NPKC), 165

National Student Center of Thailand, 109

National Student Federation of Thailand, 165

Nawaphon, 108, 111

Netiwit "Frank" Chotiphatphaisal, 65

New Rulings on the Death of King Rama VIII, 155–56

Newte, Frank Richard, 30, 31, 32, 41

Nhat Hanh, Thich (Thay), 3, 4, 77, 80, 105, 117, 119, 121, 129, 139, *184,* 186, 188–200, 215, 217, 238

Nidhi Eoseewong, 53–54, 107, 227

Nietzsche, Friedrich, 57

Nilchawee Pattanothai (Sulak's wife), 57, *58,* 59, *62,* 63, 65, 70, 115, 116, *118,* 119, 120, 137, 167, 213, 221, 223–24, 225

Niwano, Nikkyo, 214

Niwano Peace Foundation, 181

Nixon, Richard, 45

Nu'man, Sheikh Abdullah, 213–14

Nyanasamvara, Sangharaja Phra, *212,* 213

O

Olson, Grant, 76, 81

Om Mani Padme Hung, 217, 218

Oxford University, 29, 39

P

Paisan Visalo (Paisal Wongworawisit), 104, 105, 106, 123, 129, 169

Pajarayasara (Teacher of All Teachers), 65

Pakpring Thongyai, 54

Pali Text Society, 33

Parallax Press, 171, 193, 194

Parliament of the World's Religions, 216

The Path of Compassion, 193

Payutto, Prayudh, *67,* 73, 76, 80–82, 85, 128, 146

Peace Brigades International, 105, 123

Peace Research Institute Oslo, 174

People's Party, 5, 16

Pha Mong Dam, 98–100, 102

Phan Fa Bridge, 179

Phibun (Plaeak Phibunsongkram), 6, 8–9, 23, 43, 44, 90, 150

Phillips, Herbert, 51, 63, 120

Phongpaichit, Pasuk, 15–16, 44, 78, 112

Pibhop Dhongchai, 2, 65, 104, 106, 141, 168, 169, 222

Plaeak Phibunsongkram. *See* Phibun

Plato, 30, 158

Plum Village, 191, 196

Pol Pot, 108

Pond, Peter L., 140

Poonsuk Banomyong, 155

Powers That Be, 31, 93, 156–57

Pracha Hutanuwatr, 105, 107, 135, 169, *212,* 213, 222

Prajadhipok, Rama VII, King, 4

Praphas Charusathien, 91, 109

Pravit (Sulak's brother), 12, *18,* 218

Prawase Wasi, 2

Prayut Chan-o-cha, *220,* 233, 243

Pridi Banomyong, 5, 7, 8, 21, 23, 24–25, 29, 31, 154–58, *162,* 163

Princeton University, 188

Social Science Review, 42, 43, 51–55, 65,
72–73, 76, 80–83, 85, 90, 92, 103, 154
Student Edition, 66, 86
Society of Buddhist-Christian Studies,
120
Socrates, 30
Sombath Somphone, 3
Somboon (Moo) Chungprempree, 229,
230, 241
Somdet To, 28, 224
Southeast Asia Treaty Organization
(SEATO), 47
Spinoza, Baruch, 33
Spirit in Education Movement (SEM),
124, 141, 181, 224, 233
Stanton, Edwin F., 117
Stanton, Josephine, 117
St. Mary's, 7
Streckfuss, David, 122, 152, 169, 227–28
Student Christian Center, 65–66
Suan Mokkh, *74, 75,* 76, *205,* 209
Suchat Sawatsri, 85
Suchinda Kraprayoon, 1, 164–66, 177–80
Suksit Siam, 59, 61, *62,* 63, 65, 104, 107,
116
Sulak Sivaraksa. *See also individual
projects and writings*
alcohol and, 222
alternative education and, 124–25,
228
at Assumption College, 20–21, 23,
27
awards received by, 181, *182,* 183
birth of, 4–5
Black May and, 179
childhood of, *6,* 7–12
constitutional assembly and, 93–94
death and, 198–99, 218–19, 221–22,
224–26
democracy and, 30–31
development and, 46–47, 100–101,

103, 128–29
ecumenical attitude of, 129–30
as editor of the *Social Science
Review,* 51–55, 72–73, 76, 80–83,
85, 92
eightieth birthday of, 197–200, 203,
226
in exile, 1–4, 116–17, 119–26, 168–
69, 171, 177, 179
health of, 222
hospitalization of, 221–25
independent thinking and, 5, 22, 66
introduction to Buddhism for,
11–12
journals of, 134–35
kalyana-mittata (spiritual
friendship) and, 71, 185–88,
194–95, 225, 231
legacy of, 225–28
lèse-majesté charges against, 1–2,
153–54, 159–61, 164, 165–69,
170, 171, 180–81, 230, 243–45
loneliness and, 121–22, 187
mantras and, 217, 218, 222
marriage of Nilchawee and, 57,
58, 59
meditation practice of, 20, 33, 119,
121, 192, 217, 235
memory of, 134
mindful breathing and, 177
in miscellaneous photos, *26, 42, 60,
62, 64, 67, 68, 74, 102, 114, 118,
136, 144, 162, 173, 184, 201,
212, 216,* 220
monarchy and, 16–17, 30–31, 112–
13, 148, 151, 153–54, 155, 157–59,
166, 168–69, 231, 233, 244
NGO movement and, 96
as novice monk, 12–15, 17, *18,*
19–20
organizations and projects started

About the Author

Matteo Pistono is a writer and meditation teacher. His other books include *Meditation: Coming to Know Your Mind, Fearless in Tibet: The Life of the Mystic Tertön Sogyal,* and his memoir *In the Shadow of the Buddha: One Man's Journey of Discovery in Tibet.* Matteo holds a master of arts degree in Indian philosophy from the School of Oriental and African Studies at the University of London. After working with the Smithsonian Institution in Washington, DC, on Tibetan cultural programs, Matteo lived and traveled throughout the Himalayas for a decade, bringing to the West graphic accounts and photos of China's human rights abuses in Tibet. His writing and photography have appeared in the *Washington Post,* BBC News, *Men's Journal, Kyoto Journal, Buddhadharma: The Practitioner's Quarterly,* Tricycle.org, and elsewhere. Matteo lives in California with his wife and dog.

About North Atlantic Books

North Atlantic Books (NAB) is an independent, nonprofit publisher committed to a bold exploration of the relationships between mind, body, spirit, and nature. Founded in 1974, NAB aims to nurture a holistic view of the arts, sciences, humanities, and healing. To make a donation or to learn more about our books, authors, events, and newsletter, please visit www.northatlanticbooks.com.

North Atlantic Books is the publishing arm of the Society for the Study of Native Arts and Sciences, a 501(c)(3) nonprofit educational organization that promotes cross-cultural perspectives linking scientific, social, and artistic fields. To learn how you can support us, please visit our website.